Susan Carter, the Orphan Girl
by Susan Carter (Fict.Name.)

Address:
HardPress
8345 NW 66TH ST #2561
MIAMI FL 33166-2626
USA
Email: info@hardpress.net

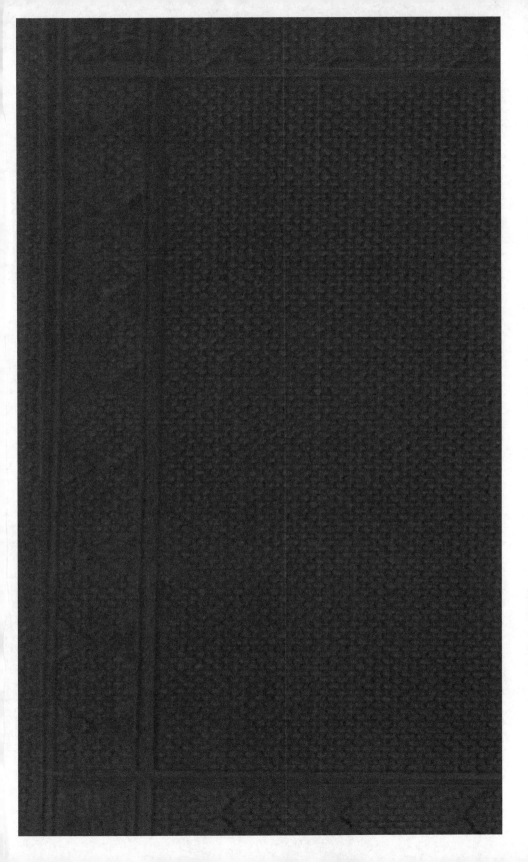

Page 58.

SUSAN CARTER,

THE

ORPHAN GIRL.

PUBLISHED UNDER THE DIRECTION OF
THE COMMITTEE OF GENERAL LITERATURE AND EDUCATION,
APPOINTED BY THE SOCIETY FOR PROMOTING
CHRISTIAN KNOWLEDGE.

LONDON:

SOCIETY FOR PROMOTING CHRISTIAN KNOWLEDGE.
SOLD AT THE DEPOSITORIES,
77, GREAT QUEEN STREET, LINCOLN'S INN FIELDS;
4, ROYAL EXCHANGE;
16, HANOVER STREET, HANOVER SQUARE;
AND BY ALL BOOKSELLERS.

PREFACE.

THE following little tale has been written from characters still living. The Author's only view in publishing it is to show, from the evidence of real life, the blessings of a religious education, even in the lowest station : that it alone can make good servants, as well as good masters and mistresses—good husbands and good wives; and that, by its means, the humblest persons are enabled, by the influence they exercise on those around them, to do as much good in their proper sphere of action, as those who have the greatest worldly gifts at their disposal.

CONTENTS.

CHAPTER I.

CHAPTER II.

CHAPTER III.

CHAPTER IV.

CHAPTER V.

SUSAN CARTER,

THE ORPHAN GIRL.

CHAPTER I.

Death of Susan's Parents.—She is placed in the Female Orphan Asylum by Mr. Harvey, the Rector of the Parish.—Her conduct there.

SUSAN CARTER was left an orphan at a very early age; her father was a sailor, and was lost at sea, and his poor wife, who was always delicate, and who was only just recovering from her third confinement, never left the house afterwards. The blow came upon her already weakened nerves, without any preparation, and her tender frame sank under it.

This was before my time; but I have often heard the Rev. Mr. Harvey speak of her meek submission, and her earnest and unceasing prayer that the 'Father of the fatherless,' and 'the God of the widow,' might be the support of her and her children. Little did she then think how quickly she was to follow her husband; for her general health having been so long delicate, she only spoke of the pain in her side, and her incessant cough, as present hindrances to her doing much towards her livelihood; but to those who saw her day by day, it was plainly told that the brightness of her eye, and the fixed hectic colour on her otherwise pallid cheek, were the treacherous marks of that disease which, in this our land, calls so many of the young and loved ones from this world.

It was only one week before she died, that, being unable to get up, as she usually did, in the middle of the day, she sent for Mr. Harvey, to beg he would come and administer to her the sacrament. He immediately went; and on his arrival, she said, in a low weak tone, 'I did not wish, Sir, to have caused you this trouble; I had hoped (and here a faint sigh escaped her, and a tear trickled down her cheek) to have knelt again at the altar of your church, and there to have partaken of the holy sacrament; but, Sir, I feel this is not to be, and that I am slowly, but surely, sinking into the grave. I had hoped, but . . .'

Here she seemed so exhausted, that Mr. Harvey begged her to let him talk, and though he never told me the particulars of his share of the conversation, I can well believe it to have been of such a consolatory nature, that from her heart she said, 'God's will be done.' 'My orphans will be His, and He will be their Father.'

After receiving the Lord's Supper, the suffering widow looked at Mr. Harvey with the meek complacency of a resigned Christian; but looks of thankfulness were all that she could then bestow, so completely was she exhausted. He remained with her for half an hour, now and then repeating a short prayer, to which she faintly said, 'Amen.' As he rose to leave the room, and took her gently by the hand, she again tried to speak, but, 'My children!' was all that she could say. Mr. Harvey assured her, that in his lifetime they should never want a friend, and, promising to call the next day, he departed; but he never saw Mrs. Carter more. During the whole of the week, until the morning of her death, she remained in so weak a state, that no one, except the friends who kindly waited on her, was permitted to see her.

After poor Mrs. Carter's funeral, the first thing to be considered was, how the children were to be provided for. Susan was then only six years of age. William (the only boy) was but four; and the infant, who was christened 'Mary,' after its poor mother, on the day of the funeral, was not five months old. Of this poor babe, the grand-mother on its father's side cheerfully undertook the charge, but one twelvemonth terminated its existence; for, having inherited disease from its mother, the poor little creature never enjoyed a day's health. A sister of Mrs. Carter's, who had a large family, said she would willingly take charge of Willy; 'for,' she said, 'one child more will be very little more trouble, and as to its bit of meat, we shall never miss it among our own little ones.'

But what was to be done with Susan? There were no other relatives near at hand, and the grandmother and aunt had made as large an offer as they could. It at once struck Mr. Harvey that perhaps he might get her into one of those asylums for the relief of suffering humanity with which this Christian land abounds. The Female Orphan Asylum, near Westminster Bridge, London, was the one he determined to try first, and he directly got cards printed, stating Susan Carter's age and the circumstances she was in, 'without father or mother, and entirely dependent on charity.'

Most fortunately, through the active exertions of Mr. Harvey and his friends, on the following election-day Susan was chosen to fill up one of the vacancies which had occurred. Poor little Susan! often has she spoken to me of the day when she kissed her brother and her baby-sister, and, with a sobbing heart, bid them good-bye!

The first thing which dried up her tears, when she arrived at the large house, which was then to be her home, was the sight of the new clothes which had been provided for her. A plain dark-blue stuff frock, white tippet, and neat cap, was the dress of the young orphans; and when Susan was dressed, and introduced into the school-room, where all her young companions were assembled, she ran up to a little girl about her own size, saying, 'You will be my sister, won't you?' The matron told her that all of them would be her sisters, for they all loved each other. 'And I will love them, too,' said Susan; and so I doubt not she did, for she was a great favourite with them all. If any of them were ill, Susan was sure to be seen running to their bedsides when school was over. If any one was in disgrace, Susan was

certain to be the one to intercede for them. Was
there any work to be finished, Susan was certain
to be the helper. And when medals and books
were given as prizes, you might be sure that
Susan's name was on the list of those to be re-
warded.

Mr. Harvey never went to London without
seeing his little orphan child, and the matron was
never tired of talking of all Susan's good qualities.

'She is no trouble, Sir,' she would say : 'indeed,
she saves me work which otherwise I must do, for
she is so orderly and so attentive, and the girls are
so fond of her, that if it is only to have Susan for
their friend, they will be good. Then, too, Sir, she
is the best reader and worker in the school, and no
one says the Catechism or understands it better
than she does. Often do I hear her say, when
the girls are inclined to speak unkindly of others,
or not willing to help each other—'You know,' she
says, ' we are to hurt nobody by *word* or deed, and
we are not to bear malice or hatred in our hearts.
It is of no use our saying our Catechism on
Sundays, if we forget it the rest of the week.' And
then if one of them happens to say a cross word,
and tell her that she is *over* good, she will say so
meekly, 'Oh ! no, dear, I am not ; but you know
I ought to keep my tongue from evil speaking,
and try to do my duty in that state of life in
which God has placed me.''

Thus would the matron talk to Mr. Harvey.
Indeed, I might fill a book with school anecdotes
of her.

CHAPTER II.

Being fourteen years old, Susan leaves the Asylum, and
     enters the service of Mrs. Harvey. — Advantages
     enjoyed by Servants in Christian Families.

EIGHT years rolled away, and Susan became then
fourteen, the age at which the girls usually left
the Asylum; but, before she did so, she, with some
other girls, were to be confirmed, it being a rule of
the institution that no girl should leave it without
enjoying the privilege of this holy ordinance. The
clergyman of the Asylum was very kind in ex-
plaining to Susan the solemn vows which she
would then have to take upon herself; those very
vows which her godfathers and godmothers had
made for her at her baptism, and which it was now
her duty to ratify. He pointed out to her that if
it had so happened that they had undertaken for
her that she should, when of fit age, fulfil certain
conditions in order that she might inherit some
great *worldly* possession, how gladly would she do
it, and how much more anxious should she be to
confirm those promises made in her name, which
had made her a ' member of Christ, a child of God,
and an inheritor of the kingdom of Heaven.' He
pointed out to her the importance of her afterwards
appearing as a communicant at the Lord's Table,
and not merely once or twice a year, but as her

bounden duty, 'at all times and in all places,' when the holy feast was prepared. She learned from him to consider it as a high and blessed privilege to be admitted thereto, and not, as too many, alas! consider it, as too *serious* a thing to have any *serious* thoughts given to it. He taught her to look forward to the continued partaking of this holy rite as a means of grace peculiarly fitted to sustain and strengthen the inner man in the conflicts which every Christian has to encounter in his earthly pilgrimage; and, above all, he impressed upon her, in an earnest and solemn tone, (which Susan had often said she could never forget,) that it was the dying command of her Saviour—of Him who gave up his life for her and all mankind,—appointed 'for the *continual* remembrance of his death.' 'Recollect, therefore,' he added, 'that so long as you wish to be considered a Christian, so long will you diligently (putting aside all excuses and pretences) attend this holy ordinance.'

By the rules of the school, Susan had to be bound for five years as a servant; and during that time, the lady into whose service she might enter had to provide her with clothes, but no wages; and, at the end of the five years, if she could bring a good character from her mistress, the gentlemen of the Asylum would present her with five guineas.

Poor Susan! it was a painful thing to her to know that she must soon say Good-bye to her young companions, who, from the youngest to the eldest, all loved her.

'I shall never be able to say my lessons perfectly without Susan to hear me first,' said one ; and 'I shall often be kept in school to do my sampler,' said another, 'for I can never do it unless Susan is by my side.' And 'who will help us out of disgrace when we have behaved ill?' said a third. In short, one and all were discovering that any one could have been spared better than Susan.

The matron, too, looked quite sad when she spoke of the day being fixed for Susan to leave the Asylum; and as to poor Susan herself, the tears would stream from her eyes, if the subject was but named ; but, in spite of all these lamentations, the dreaded day did arrive, and Susan, laden with little remembrances from her young companions, and a neat little book called 'Bishop Wilson's Sacra Privata,' from the matron, set off for B—ton Rectory, and became the servant of her kind friends Mr. and Mrs. Harvey. Her place was to take charge of the younger children ; and long after she had left, Mrs. Harvey used to talk of her handy little Susan, and many a time did she express a wish to meet with another 'Susan.' She was so cheerful and willing to do anything in her power to help any one in the house, so quick in getting her own work done, and so useful in instructing the children in reading and saying their hymns, and still more in impressing on their minds those religious instructions which their mother first instilled into them; and then, happily, she was seen to practise herself what she taught them. She did not say to the children, 'You must never tell a story,' and then go and practise deceit herself. She did not do one thing in her mistress's presence, and another in her absence, but showed in all her actions that she was serving her employers, 'Not with eye service, as men pleasers, but in singleness of heart, fearing God.'

I have often thought that there are few stations in life where more real comfort and independence may be enjoyed, than by domestic servants in a well-regulated Christian family. Everything is provided for them—lodging, food, and raiment. They have no 'care for the morrow' thrust upon them. Oftentimes, when the head of a family sits down to his daily meal, prepared for him with comfort, perhaps with luxury, does he do so with a troubled and thoughtful spirit; while the servant, standing behind his chair, has, or may have, a heart as 'light as air.' Work they have to do, and miserable is he who has none. Sometimes it may press heavily upon them, but there is no burden upon the mind. An occasional excess of bodily fatigue seems, in the common course of things, to be about the extent of the evil to which their calling subjects them, in a sober and well-regulated family.

Thus did Susan Carter find her condition of servitude. She had the happiness of living in a kind and Christian family, and her days passed in contentment and thankfulness.

CHAPTER III.

Susan goes to London.—Her reception at the Female
    Orphan Asylum.—Appears before the Committee.—
    Receives a reward for her good conduct. — Her
    intentions as to the disposal of her money.

THE time now arrived for her appearing before
the gentlemen of the Committee at the Asylum
in London; and it was with a beating heart that
she got on the top of the coach that was to take
her there, carrying in her pocket the following
testimonial from her mistress:—

    'Mrs. Harvey has much pleasure in informing
the Committee of the Asylum for Female Orphans,
that Susan Carter has, during the five years of her
residence in her family, given her the most entire
satisfaction, and that she considers her a most
faithful and trustworthy servant, and well deserv-
ing of the reward usually given by the Asylum.'

    When the coach set her down at the Asylum
gates, her legs could scarcely carry her fast enough
to the door; and when she got there, she felt so
agitated, that it was some minutes before she had
strength enough to ring the bell. At last she
gave a strong pull; and a girl (whom she had
left a *little* one, but who was now grown almost
as big as herself) opened the door.

    'Can I see the matron?' said she, not reco-
gnising, in the tall stout girl, *little* Mary Hales.

'She is very busy just now,' said the girl; 'but step in, and if you will tell me your name, I will let her know, for she is seeing the room made ready for our Committee gentlemen, who are going to give the rewards to twelve of our girls, who have been five years in their places; and Susan Carter is coming, and Mary Andrews, and Susan Bell and—but I can't recollect all the names; perhaps you are one?' And, as she said this, she looked her earnestly in the face, saying, 'Why, you *are* Susan Carter, I am sure, for that is her smile; but you looked so rosy when you first came to the door, that I did not know you again.'

'And I am sure,' said Susan, 'I never thought the great tall girl who opened the door was Mary Hales, whom I left such a little creature; but I forget how many years it is since I said, Good bye to you all. But where is Mrs. Wilson, our good, kind matron? I trust she is still here.'

Mary did not wait for a reply, but ran off to fetch her. She presently arrived, and I need not say how joyful the meeting was on both sides, nor need I dwell on Susan's rushing into the school-room, and the many affectionate greetings which she had among her old school-fellows; but I must tell you how frightened she was at having to appear before the gentlemen, sitting round a large table covered with green cloth, who had met to read the testimonials and present the rewards. However, the matron kindly took her into the room, and after a little time she felt less flurried; her cheeks resumed their natural colour, and when

B 2

she presented her mistress's letter, and saw the gentlemen smile with approbation as they read it, she began to think how silly she had been to be frightened.

Out of twelve girls who presented themselves, there was only one who had proved unworthy of the reward, and she was described by her mistress as being thoughtless, pert, and dissatisfied with the clothes she had found for her. To her the gentlemen first addressed themselves in words of severe reproof, telling her how grieved they were that any girl brought up in that Asylum should be sent back with such a character; but by way of inducing her to reform, they said that, if she could prevail on her mistress to keep her another year, and at the end of that time she could bring an amended character, they would present her with two guineas. 'Not,' said they, 'to spend in dress, but as a little beginning to lay by in the Savings Bank.'

At this Sarah Dawson (for that was her name) tossed her head on one side, and muttered something which was not audible to the gentlemen, but which made Susan blush for her. The gentlemen, having examined their testimonials, presented five guineas to each of the eleven girls, charging them to put by a *part*, if not the whole of it, in a Savings Bank. As the money was put into Susan's hand, she looked very pleased. She had never possessed so much money before. She had fifteen shillings in the Savings Bank, which had been given her in small sums, and she wanted to raise money enough to bind her brother to some trade ; for, though her aunt had kept him all this time, and Mr. Harvey had put him to school, she knew that the former could not afford to pay ten pounds for his apprenticeship; 'and now,' thought she, 'I have six pounds to give to my aunt for my brother, and he can be bound apprentice to John James, the shoemaker, or Thomas Simpson, the joiner, or any other one he likes.'

Nothing moves so rapidly as thought. Susan was scarcely out of the Committee-room before all this had passed through her mind on the sight of the money ; and she was so busy thinking over the joy she should have in going to her aunt's, when she returned home, that the matron had to touch her shoulder in order to get an answer to some question she was putting to her, as to whether she was likely to remain in her situation.

'Indeed, I hope so, ma'am,' said Susan. 'Master is so good to me, and, indeed, to all of us, that if I were to leave him, I believe I should never get such another : and mistress is the mildest lady I ever saw ; I don't believe she could *scold* us; though, when we do wrong, she always tells us of it ; but then she says at the same time, in such a sweet way, 'Well, Susan, don't look so unhappy about it ; we all have our faults, and if you strive to correct them, that is all I expect ; I don't look for perfection in you or any one else.''

'You have been a lucky girl, Susan,' said

Mrs. Wilson, 'to get into such a family; it is a blessing which you cannot duly feel till a few more years are over your head, and then you will see the dangers you have escaped by living with such people. Of course you go to church on a Sunday?'

'Oh, yes! mistress manages that we should all go once a-day, and some of us twice a-day; but where there is a young baby, one of us must be at home both morning and afternoon. We are not allowed to go out visiting on a Sunday, though with many families about it is the custom to do so. Our last new housemaid was not very well pleased when she found that this was one of the rules of the house; but mistress soon convinced her that going from house to house, paying visits, was *not* 'keeping holy the Sabbath day;' and, as we are all allowed to have one afternoon in a week in turn, we do not think this rule any hardship. Then master or mistress always hears us read a chapter or two on Sunday evening, and explains it to us, and questions us on it, so that we pass our Sundays very pleasantly, as well as profitably.'

'Ah! my dear Susan,' said Mrs. Wilson, 'may it always be your lot to follow those ways which are 'ways of pleasantness,' and those paths which are 'paths of peace.' You know, Susan, where alone these are to be found.'

'I should be unworthy of this Asylum, and above all, of you, our dear good matron, had I not long ago learned that—

' 'Tis Religion that can give
 Sweetest pleasure whilst we live ;
 And 'tis Religion can supply
 Sweetest comfort when we die.'

'Yes, Susan, you are right; in youth, woman-
hood, or old age, religion is our best friend, and
the Bible our best instructor. You have known
the pleasure it affords in health and in youth, and
I trust you will find it your comforter whenever
you are called upon to share in the trials of this
world. It was the consolation of your mother's
dying hours, as your master, I know, has told
you.'

Poor Susan's heart was too full to speak, but
that she *had* afterwards her trials, and that the
Bible *was* the comforter of her joys and sorrows,
my readers shall hereafter be made acquainted, if
they have the patience to read a brief account of
them.

CHAPTER IV.

Mrs. Harvey gives Susan some good advice.—Its effects upon her.—Susan's anxiety about her Brother.—How he is provided for.—Her conduct towards her Aunt.

AFTER going once more into the school-room to shake hands with all her former companions, and running up stairs into the dormitory, (for so the bed-rooms of the Asylum were called,) to see the bed which for so many years she had nightly occupied, and peeping into the rooms where their Sunday clothes were all so neatly arranged on shelves, with the number over each, (for every girl on entering the school was called by a number instead of by name,) and hastily running into the kitchen and laundry, where she had learned so much that was useful, Susan once more went to Mrs. Wilson, and bidding her good-bye, she set off to meet the coach, to take her to B——ton, (for that was the village of which her master was rector.)

When Susan reached home, she directly went to her mistress to thank her for the character she had given her, and showed her the five guineas which had been presented to her. 'And now, ma'am,' she said, 'I want master to be so kind as to see about getting my brother bound to some trade. I believe it will cost ten pounds, and I know that my aunt cannot afford to pay all that sum, and I am so pleased that I can now help her to pay for my brother, for she has been quite a mother to him. I think he wishes to be a shoemaker; but when you can spare me, ma'am, I will walk over to my aunt's and inquire whether he has finally settled.'

'You may do so to-morrow,' said her mistress, pleased to see such thoughtfulness in one so young; 'but do you think you can spare all your own money? will you not require some of it for your own clothes; for you know I shall no longer find you clothes, but shall give you wages instead— that is to say, if you wish to remain with me?'

Susan coloured up very much, and tried to say something about her mistress being pleased to keep, her and Mrs. Harvey then continued, 'Well, Susan, if *you* are *pleased* to stay, and *I* am *pleased* to keep you, the next thing to be settled is, what wages I am to give you. The sum I propose to offer you at present is six pounds per year. Now, this will not allow of any finery in dress, but it will find you everything that is necessary for your station, and allow of your laying by also a little every quarter; but before you part with your six pounds, remember you will receive no more for three months; so it is for you to decide whether you can go without any money for that time.'

'Oh,' said Susan, 'I believe I shall require nothing new for a much longer time, thanks to you, ma'am; and as to finery, if I were buying any, I believe the recollection of my neat orphan dress would reproach me, and I should fancy it saying to me, 'Is it this you were taught when you wore for so many years your dark stuff frock, and neat cap and tippet?' and, indeed, ma'am, I do so love my old dress, that if it were not that it would look singular, I should like always to wear it.'

'Well, Susan, though you cannot wear that, you can always dress equally plainly, and I would strongly advise you not to be led by *example*, of which you have but too many, to dress beyond your station. If ever you are tempted to envy the gay ribbons and expensive shawls of your acquaintance, just calculate how much you suppose they cost, and if you have as much money, take it at once to the Savings Bank, and reflect that hereafter you will derive more comfort from it, (particularly if you should marry or be ill,) than any shawl or ribbon could afford you.'

Susan thanked her mistress for her good advice, (which, I believe, she never forgot,) and went to tell her fellow-servants of her day's proceedings. Susan was a favourite with all the servants; for though her exactness in following the orders of her master and mistress, and her determination in opposing anything contrary to their interest, often prevented them from doing otherwise, yet she never treated them as if she was superior to them on that account, but obtained their good opinion by her own consistent conduct, and their affection by her readiness to assist any of them when her own work was finished. Her present joy was shared, therefore, by all her fellow-servants; and one of them thought she could now afford herself a silk gown for visiting in, (for they all knew that her mistress would not allow one to be worn in the house.)

The lady's maid hoped she would now treat herself to a bit of edging on her caps; and the housemaid begged, now that she was her own mistress in dress, she would not grudge herself a bow for her cap.

Susan heard patiently their kind wishes, and then laughingly said, 'I am sorry to disappoint you all, but my money will be very shortly spent, though not, I assure you, on myself.'

They then began, each in turn, to inquire what she meant to do with it, but after all their guesses, no one could discover how the five guineas were to be spent, and Susan would not satisfy them that night, but promised to do so the following one.

The next day Susan forgot two or three little things which it was her place to do; but her mistress kindly took no notice, as she saw that it was the afternoon's pleasure which was uppermost in her thoughts; and as soon as she had finished her morning's walk, she said to her, 'There, Susan, you need not wait for the children's dinner; I will attend to them; I see you are longing to take your riches to your aunt.'

Susan could have jumped for joy, and she instantly ran and put on her neat straw bonnet, and pinning her shawl on as she went down stairs, she walked as fast as she could to her aunt's cottage.

Her aunt was busy, washing, and looked up not a little surprised to see her niece so early in the day.

'Well, Susan, dear, what has brought you here so early? We were talking of you only last night, and wishing we could see you, to be the first to tell you the good news.'

'What good news can you have to tell me, aunt? I have some to tell you, but I was not thinking of hearing any from you; but do tell me what it is?'

'No, no,' said her aunt, 'I am the oldest, so age before honesty, if you please; let me hear your news first.'

'Well, then,' said Susan, putting her hand in her pocket, and pulling out a little parcel, which she began unfolding, (for it was carefully inclosed in many pieces of paper,) until at last she came to the sovereigns,—'there are six sovereigns for you, aunt, to go towards my brother's apprenticeship. I know you cannot afford to pay for him, and when I get my wages, I hope every quarter to give you a trifle, until I make up the ten pounds.'

Her aunt could not speak for a few moments, from amazement, and then said, 'My dear Susan, where did you get this money?'

Susan briefly told her of the kindness of the gentlemen in giving her five guineas, and of her having saved the remainder in small sums which different ladies had given her. 'And now, aunt,' said she, 'I am so pleased that I can help you to

Page 28.

provide for my brother;' and in saying this, she put out her hand to place the money in her aunt's, who pushed it from her, saying, 'No, my dear Susan, your brother is provided for by one who can better spare the money than you.'

'Not by you, aunt, I am sure; for I know how difficult it has been for you to bring him up with your children, and I know of no relation who could help you.'

'No relation, indeed, Susan; but one who has ever been to me and mine *more* than a relation— it is *your* master.'

'My master!' said Susan, now in her turn surprised; 'has he, then, been giving you the money?'

Not exactly that; but he has paid it to John James for me, and told me I might send your brother to begin work to-day. Poor boy! he set off in high spirits, and has already been calculating on mending our shoes in his spare hours; yes, yours too, Susan.'

'But how much has my master paid?' said Susan.

'That I cannot tell you, for it did not become me to ask any questions after having received such a favour.'

Poor Susan scarcely knew how to believe all that she heard; this, then, was her aunt's *good news*. How strange, she thought, that her mistress had not told her of this; and then again she thought that, perhaps, her mistress did not know it; and now she was just as anxious to run home, and thank her master, as she had before been to come and see her aunt; but this her aunt would not allow, but insisted on her having both dinner and tea with her; and during that time, after much persuasion, Susan did prevail on her to accept one sovereign to buy a gown for herself and frocks for her children. As soon as she had finished tea, she set off to go home; and immediately went to her master to thank him for his great kindness to her brother.

He merely told her that he had done it in performance of his promise to her mother, on her dying bed; 'and I trust,' said he, 'that both of you will realize the anxious wishes which she so often expressed to me for you.'

Though Susan had but a slight recollection of her mother, the mention of her name never failed to bring tears into her eyes. They were not exactly tears of sorrow, for there was much of gratitude and thankfulness mingled with the feeling of grief which the loss of a parent, at whatever period of our existence, must ever afterwards call forth. She always felt how completely she had experienced that 'the Father of the fatherless' had been truly hers, and that the orphan's cry had been heard by her God.

Her master, seeing her affected, changed the subject, and said, 'I dare say you will already have formed some plan for your six pounds; tell me what it is.'

'Why, sir, if you please, I should like to put my five pounds into the Savings Bank.'

'I thought your mistress told me that you had six pounds.'

'So I had, sir,' said Susan, blushing: 'but——' and she hesitated to go on.

'But what, Susan? I hope you have not spent it in any way that you are ashamed to own to me.'

'No, sir, not ashamed; but——I gave it to my aunt to buy a gown for herself and frocks for the children; she has always been kind to me, sir, and been quite a mother to my brother.'

'You are a good girl, Susan, not to forget the kindness of your aunt; and I am pleased that, by my having paid for your brother, I have enabled you to make this little present to her, which I am sure would be acceptable.'

Susan feared that she was taking up too much of her master's time; so again thanking him for his goodness, and assuring him that she should never forget it, she left the room.

When Susan went into the nursery, she found her mistress there, hearing the children say their prayers; but after they had finished, and were in bed, her mistress asked her (with a smile) how her aunt liked her proposal.

'Why, indeed, ma'am, master had been before me, and paid the money for my brother, so I could only get my aunt to take one pound, and I have now five pounds to put in the Savings Bank. I am sure master is the most generous gentleman in the world; and then he does it all so quietly, and no one about him is a bit the wiser. I dare say, ma'am, you did not know of what he had done when you sent me to my aunt?'

'Yes, I did, Susan; but I would not deprive *you* of the pleasure of offering the money to your aunt, nor *her* of the pleasure of seeing your thoughtfulness. I hope your brother will be steady, and attend to his trade, and then there is no fear of his being able to make a livelihood, without being a burden to his aunt.'

CHAPTER V.

Susan and her Fellow-servants.—Conversation on Savings Banks.

SUSAN sat busily at work, thinking over all that had happened during the last two days, with a thankful heart, when Sally the housemaid came to call her to supper. Susan had a small piece of sewing to do to complete her job, when Sally called, and she did not move immediately, 'Now, Susan, child, do come; we are all waiting for you.'

'Don't wait for me, Sally dear; I will be down as soon as I have finished Missis's petticoat.'

'Well, but, Susan, do come now; for we are all *so* anxious to hear about your money.'

Susan then remembered her promise the preceding evening, of telling them how she meant to

spend her money; but her plans were now quite
changed. 'Here she comes, here she comes!'
were the words she heard as she went down stairs,
and she could not help laughing as she entered
the kitchen.

'Come, Susan, come, and let's have your story,
for I know you will have a long one to tell
about your five guineas,' said Lucy, 'and lots of
good advice into the bargain; come now, give
us the sermon first, and then we can have the
story afterwards.'

'Now, indeed,' said Susan, 'you are quite
wrong, for I have *no* sermon, and but a short
story for you, as my money has not been wanted
as I expected. I intended to have given it to
my aunt, to pay the expenses of my brother's
apprenticeship, but our good master had already
done so, and out of my little store my aunt would
only take one sovereign, so that the remaining
five pounds I have given to my master to place
in the Savings Bank for me.'

'Why, Susan, thou art a clever lass,' said the
cook, 'to give away one pound out of five, and
yet have five pounds left; do tell us what new
way of reckoning this is; it may be useful to me
when I make up my accounts.'

'You forget, cook,' said Susan, 'that I had
fifteen shillings in the Savings Bank, which different kind ladies have given me, and the gentlemen
gave me five *guineas*. Miss Simpson, you know,
gave me half-a-crown for some work I did for
her, and little Miss Lizzy gave me a shilling

c

for washing her doll's clothes, and mistress gave me two shillings for a cap ribbon, but said I might keep the money, if I preferred it; and so I did; and in this way, you see, my shillings quickly increased.'

'But, my dear Susan,' said Sally, 'why not keep the five pounds yourself? Perhaps you will be seeing something you want, and then you will have no money to buy it with, and you may not like to get it out when your master has put it in.'

'I am quite sure, Sally, that I shall see nothing that I *want*. I may very likely see something I may *fancy*, and if I am likely to yield to my *fancy*, why it is quite as well that it is out of my power to do so.'

'Now, that's just like you,' said Sally; 'I'm sure I have been ten years in place, and never saved twelve-pence yet, and never shall, I believe.'

'The more's the pity,' said Susan, 'for you know not how soon you may want it.'

'Oh,' said Sally, tossing her head, 'I suppose you mean I don't know how soon I may be married, and that's true enough; but if I am not worth marrying *without* money, no one shall have me, I assure you.'

'I was not thinking about your marrying,' said Susan, quietly, 'though it may be *worth* your consideration; but how many other things may cause you to wish you had had a little forethought! Suppose you were to have a long illness, and were obliged to leave your place? or met with

an accident, and were to break your arm or leg?
or suppose your poor widowed mother should be
bed-ridden, and you, her own daughter, for whom
she has toiled day and night to place you in a
situation to enable you to gain a livelihood, not
able to give her a shilling or two a week to pro-
cure any little comforts for her.'

'But, Susan,' said Sally, 'you are so fond of
supposing this, and *supposing* that, and after all,
not one of your *supposings* may come to pass.'

'But, dear Sally, have I supposed anything very
unlikely? Can you not at this moment think of
similar cases to all those I have mentioned? Has
not Mary Harrison been six months confined to
her room, and likely to be as many more? and is
it not now her greatest comfort to think she is
not a burden to her mother? And is not Susan
Hall, the Squire's kitchen-maid, laid up with a
broken collar-bone, from falling down some high
steps? And has not poor Peggy Pattison been
bed-ridden these three years? and is it not from
her grand-daughter that she gets a shilling a week
to pay for a girl to wait on her?'

'There, now, did I not say,' said Lucy, (the
lady's maid,) 'that we should have a sermon from
Susan, and I am sure it has been long enough,
in all conscience!'

'Indeed, I had no intention of giving you a
sermon, as you call it; but Sally is fond of a little
debate, and as we always part good friends afterwards, I have no objection to debate with her.
c 2

So, Sally, what do you say—are your next quarter's wages to go into the Savings Bank? You know another good thing is, your money goes on increasing there, for they give interest for it. For every hundred shillings that are put into the Savings Bank, you get every year three or four shillings more.'

By this time the nursery-bell rang. Her mistress always allowed her half an hour for her supper, during which time she sat with the children herself. She did not like to prevent the servants from meeting together at their last meal, and yet wished to discourage gossiping; so that, when the half hour was expired, she always rang the bell, and Susan ran up-stairs. This night, however, poor Susan's bread and cheese had been sadly neglected, owing to the discussion, and when the bell sounded, the first mouthful had not been tasted. She hastily swallowed a few pieces, and flew up stairs, but was quite out of breath when she reached the room.

'You have been running up stairs very fast, Susan,' said her mistress. 'Do not do so in future, for I see you are rendered uncomfortable by it; a minute more or less is not important to me; and, perhaps, if you *began* to come up stairs as soon as the bell rang, you would be up just as soon as you are now.'

Susan understood her mistress's reproof. 'I beg your pardon, ma'am, I am sure; but I believe I have talked a little too much to-night, and so had not thought of my supper till the bell rang, and then I stayed to swallow a few mouthfuls.'

'Well, Susan, I hope your words have been as beneficial to your *fellow-servants* as your supper would have been to you. I need not caution you against idle gossiping and story-telling, for you know in what book 'all foolish talking' is forbidden, and I am sure you will not encourage it in my house.'

'I hope not, ma'am,' said Susan; 'our conversation to-night was about Savings Banks, and I did my best to show Sally that it was only common prudence to put our money into them.'

'You did very right, Susan; and by thus advising your fellow-servants to do what you know to be right, you may often be the means, by God's blessing, of doing them great good. If we were all of us to remember that we shall be judged hereafter, not only for what we have done, but also for what we have left *undone*, we should be more anxious to make ourselves useful to our neighbour; and in your rank of life, Susan, perhaps this is as often done in the way of conversation and example as in any other. Of all our members, none requires such constant watching as the tongue. A hasty or unkind word is so easily said; an idle story, which has little or no foundation, is so agreeable to tell, and so eagerly listened to; the faults of our neighbours are so plainly seen by us, and are so pleasing to talk of, and it is so nice to have a little piece of news, no matter of *whom*, that we are all of us too apt to offend with our tongues daily, if not hourly, against that charity which 'thinketh no evil.' But I am forgetting my supper, Susan; so good night!'

CHAPTER VI.

Sally begins to see things in a right light.—Susan gives her a valuable lesson. — James Dawes makes Susan a proposal of Marriage.—The character of James.

WHEN her mistress had gone down stairs, Susan began to think over all she had said, and she did not forget that night, in her prayers, to thank God for having given her so good and thoughtful a mistress. What a good rule it would be, if we would all of us accustom ourselves every night, when we fall down on our knees, just to recollect, independently of those general and hourly mercies for which we have so much cause to be thankful, any particular blessings for which the day past had been distinguished, and to pour out the thankfulness of our hearts accordingly!

In the kitchen, Susan's absence had caused perhaps a little more mirth than her presence. Not that anything very unkind was said of Susan, but a few foolish jests were passed upon her five pounds being in her master's keeping, and upon her having actually saved two shillings instead of buying a cap ribbon. Many remarks were made upon her being so particular and so saving; until

Sally, who had been aroused by some of the observations made by Susan at supper-time, began to take her part in her absence, which occasioned Lucy to say to her, 'Why, Sally, are you going to turn miser, too? I do believe you'll be Susan over again.'

'If that is being a miser, I wish I was one at this moment,' said Sally. 'I wonder when you, or I, or Cook, or James, or John, or many more that we know, ever gave a whole sovereign to a poor relation.'

'Well, well,' said Cook, 'don't be so hot; Lucy didn't mean to say anything against Susan, only you know she is a *little* particular.'

'She's not a *little* particular,' said Sally, somewhat tartly; 'she's *very* particular, not only in doing her own duty, but in trying to get others to do theirs.'

'Oh, then, I trust she will be successful with you, my dear!' said Lucy, with a sneer; and Sally left the kitchen, for she felt that she could not control her temper if she remained. Sally flew up stairs to the nursery; there she found Susan reading her Bible. She was waiting to be summoned to prayers, as she always attended in the evening, and Sally in the morning; so she fancied when she heard Sally enter that it was for the purpose of calling her down.

'Has the prayer-bell rung?' said Susan.

'No, not yet; but Cook and Lucy have made me so angry that I determined to leave the kitchen.'

'Well, Sally, it is better to run away from

temptation than to fall into it; and if, by changing your room, you change your angry thoughts for good ones, you are very right.'

'Why, Susan, I believe you would make any one think good thoughts.'

'Oh, Sally, don't say that! you must know from Whom it is that 'all holy thoughts and all good counsels' come; so you should not say that *I* can make any one have them.'

'Well, Susan, you know what I mean.'

'You mean, I suppose,' said Susan, 'that, by God's blessing, what I have said has sometimes been the *means* of making you think rightly.'

'Oh, Susan, how I wish I was as good as you! and yet Cook and Lucy said such cross things of you just now; it was that which made me in a passion; they said——'

Here Susan put her hand on her mouth, saying, 'Stop, Sally, a minute, and answer me one question. Is it any fault of mine of which they complain?'

'No, indeed, they could not find a fault in you; I defy them,' said Sally, all her former warmth returning.

'You are very rash, dear Sally, in your zeal for me, but, if you really love me, promise me one thing.'

'Anything you like,' said Sally.

'It is, then, that you never repeat to me any unkind thing that others may say of me behind my back, unless it is some offence I have committed against them, and then I should wish you to tell me, that I might do all in my power to repair my fault.'

'Oh, but it is so shameful, it is so untrue, it is——'

'Recollect your promise: if it is untrue, it is the more harmless; but they may think differently to-morrow. We none of us know what we say when we are in a passion.'

'I'm sure I don't,' said Sally.

'Well, then, Sally, judge others as you would wish others to judge you, and don't raise up angry feelings in any one, by repeating what others may say of them in an angry moment.'

A noise on the stairs told Susan it was prayer-time. The next morning Susan met Cook and Lucy as usual. She would not let them suppose that she had even had a hint of anything unkindly from them, and as they did really respect Susan for her goodness, and even fancied they loved her, when she did anything to help them, things went on as usual. A change, however, took place a year afterwards in the establishment of her master. Owing to the loss of some money, (though not to a considerable amount,) in a bank which had stopped payment, Mr. Harvey determined to put down his carriage, and part with his coachman and groom.

Was it merely a fancy of Mrs. Harvey's, that Susan turned very red and then very pale, when she told her that James was going to leave? And if he was rather long in returning from taking a message, or from carrying letters to the post, and her mistress began to wonder what could be detaining James, why was Susan so very ready to find out many things that might keep him? Perhaps my readers will say, 'Because Susan did to others as she would have them do to her;' and that was very true. But what was rather remarkable, her mistress observed that Susan seemed frightened to make the excuses for James, though in general she had no fear in speaking to her mistress; but this riddle was solved when James *really* went.

The state of the case was this:—Very soon after James came to live at the Rectory, he had made his proposal to Susan, but she firmly told him that she could make *no* promise till she knew more of him than she could do in so short a period.

'It is for your good, James, as well as mine,' said she, one day, 'that we should thoroughly know each other before we make so serious an engagement.'

James was rather vexed, and argued, and argued, but all to no purpose. Then he said he was sure she liked George better than him, and that he had seen her walk home from church last Sunday with him. Susan was now in her turn somewhat piqued, but tried to say *calmly*—'Well, then, James, I wonder you should wish to be engaged to me, if you think I like another person better, or even if there was a chance of my doing so afterwards. I am sure I should not wish you to engage yourself to me if I thought you liked Sally or Lucy better.'

'But you *know* I do *not.* You *know*, Susan, that I love you better than any one I ever saw.'

'So much the worse for you,' said Susan, with a suppressed smile, 'if all the time, you think I like some one else better.'

'Now, Susan, dear, you are so unkind, you will take all I say for earnest.'

'Oh! oh! then, after all, you are not in earnest. Then, Sir, good morning to you.'

In this way did Susan often tease poor James, half jesting and half in earnest; but when the time for his departure arrived, he would not leave the house without a promise that she would be his wife. He wanted her at once to fix the time—the month, at least, if not the day; but this Susan also opposed. 'Where was the money to furnish the house?' James had saved five pounds out of his wages during the last year, and Susan had by this time saved twelve pounds.

'Perhaps, then, James, in two years' time,' said Susan, 'you will have got money enough to furnish the house, and I shall have more than enough to pay the first year's rent.'

James thought Susan's money might as well go towards the furniture, and then they might get married the sooner; but Susan would not hear of this.

'No, no, James,' said she; ''marry in haste and repent at leisure,' is an old proverb, and not the less true because it is old; if you please, we will have the leisure beforehand, and so escape the *repentance* afterwards. Suppose you or I were to be ill afterwards, and not a halfpenny in the world to fall back upon; a pretty situation we should be in, and all because we would not wait a year or two longer.'

'Why, Susan, you talk just as if a year was no more than a week or a month: now do, dear, say that at the end of this year we shall be married.'

'What, do you mean at Christmas, and this is only Midsummer?'

'Yes; that will be in six months, and I am sure that is a *very* long time to wait.'

'Do you think, then, that by that time you can furnish our cottage?'

'Why, no, not quite; but perhaps in a year from this time I may be able, so will you promise me then?'

'I promise you, James, that whenever you can furnish a cottage for us to live in, I will become your wife, but not before; and mind, dear James, we must not begin with any *debts*.'

James promised her that everything should be paid for before it was sent home, and he was *quite* sure that, in a year, all would be ready. Susan thought otherwise, but she said no more at that time. The same evening James left the Rectory, but he did not leave the neighbourhood, for he went to be groom to Squire Noble, who lived about a mile off; and before he left, he asked leave of his master to come to the Rectory once a week.

His master smiled, saying, 'What, James, to come courting, eh ?'

James, a little confused, said, 'Why, sir, if it wont offend you.'

'I must first know who the lass is,' said the Rector, 'though I can give a pretty shrewd guess, I suspect; is it Susan Carter ?'

James confessed it was.

'And a good wife she'll make you,' said his master. 'I can tell you, he will be a happy man who gets her; but mind, James, she was committed to my care by her dying mother, and I will not give my consent to her marrying any one who has not a comfortable home to take her to, and the prospect of maintaining her decently.'

James assured his master that it was his earnest wish to do both for her; and having gained a favourable answer to his request, and expressed his regret at leaving his master, he bade him good-bye.

Susan took an opportunity that same evening to mention to her mistress what had passed between herself and James. At first she hesitated and stopped, and seemed much ashamed, but Mrs. Harvey helped her through with her story, as she was quite sure, for some time past, that James was trying to get Susan for his wife; and though she did not wish to lose Susan, yet she was pleased at the prospect of her marrying so steady a young man as James had appeared to be during the three years he had been at the Rectory. He was a regular attendant at church, morning and afternoon: and what was also a gratifying thing to his master

and mistress, he never absented himself from the
sacrament of the Lord's Supper, thus setting an
excellent example to all the men-servants in the
parish; and it was happily followed by a few,
though not by so many as the good Rector desired.   James always said that it was his good
mother (a widow) who was the great means of
his being a constant communicant.

'I dare not,' he would sometimes say to his
fellow-servants, 'leave a church when the Lord's
Supper is ready, and not partake of it.   My
mother's words rush to my mind, and I think I
hear her say, as she often used to do, My son, if
thy Saviour had bid thee offer some *great sacri-
fice,* perhaps one that would cost you years of
labour to perform, would you not do it in fulfil-
ment of a dying request? how much more, then,
when he asks of thee so small a thing: 'Do this
in remembrance of me;' and then she would get
closer and closer to me, and, at last, squeezing my
hand, she would say, 'Oh! James, whenever you
are tempted to leave your pew when the Minister
invites you to the altar, ask yourself this question,—Can I be sure that I shall live to see this
table again spread? and then I am sure you will
not dare to slight what may be *your* dying repast,
as it was your Saviour's.''

By similar reasonings James had prevailed on
George to become a communicant with him.   Mrs.
Harvey was well aware that to Susan and James
she owed many useful reforms in the kitchen; she
therefore told Susan that she fully approved of *her*

choice as well as James's, and the only thing they had now to consider was, the most prudent way of beginning the world. Susan told her mistress of the conditions she had imposed on James, of which she quite approved, and agreed with Susan in thinking that the period was more likely to be two years than one.

CHAPTER VII.

What is Useful, and what is Cheap ?—Hints upon Shopping.— Finery in Dress.

DURING this time Sally continued to improve under Susan's kind instructions ; and when, at the end of the first year, she found two sovereigns in the Savings Bank, she could scarcely believe it possible. The way Susan contrived to get so much of Sally's money deposited there, was by getting her to give her five or ten shillings every time she received her wages, and any little presents besides, so that Sally scarcely missed the money, and had no idea of its having amounted up to so much, for Susan always kept the book in which the sums were entered, and did not show it to Sally till the end of the first year. From the result of its being so much beyond Sally's calculation, Susan hoped to persuade her to become still more careful ; for though she was much improved in her way of spending her wages, Susan still thought that she was not quite so economical as she might be. A pretty silk handkerchief, or gauze ribbon, would sometimes tempt her to lay out a shilling or two, because they were 'so cheap.' The shopman had assured her that 'they never would be so low again;' 'that she had much better not lose such a chance;' 'that they were really giving them away,' &c.

'But did you really want the ribbon or handkerchief?' Susan would say, in her mild way.

'Why, not exactly,' said Sally.

'Well, then, don't you see that their being cheap was no advantage to you, even if you had paid only half the money that you have done; for you have spent it in things which you did not want, and therefore, had you not seen them, and listened to the nonsense which shopmen so often talk, (to call it by no harsher name,) you would now have had your money in your pocket.'

'Well, but, Susan dear, I did not buy much; you see there are only four yards, and but sixpence a yard.'

'That is to say, *only* four yards more than you wanted.'

One day, when they were thus talking over a purchase of poor Sally's, she asked Susan if she would in future go with her to lay out her wages.

'I should so like to see how you would manage, Susan dear, and what you would say when the shopman, and sometimes the master of the shop, persuades you to buy something you do not want.'

'Oh! is that a difficulty with you, Sally? I think if *that* is all, your lesson in shopping will be quickly learnt.'

The next time they received their wages, Susan took half of hers to the Savings Bank, and ten shillings of Sally's, before they laid out a farthing. They then went to buy some stockings. The man (as is too generally the custom) brought out some very slight ones. They were white.

'Have you no unbleached ones !' inquired Susan.

'Oh ! yes, we have ; but these are very much preferred by our customers.'

'I will thank you to show them to me.'

After some little trouble, she got three pairs of strong stockings : they were not so smart-looking as those which she first saw, but she knew they would last double the time, and that was always her first consideration in buying anything. She bought several other articles in the same way, and Sally saw, to her amazement, that Susan paid no regard to the opinion of the shopman, who was rather forward in giving it. At last, when she had finished making all the purchases for herse' and Sally, he brought a box of edgings. Now he hoped that he could tempt them; he had just got in a lot of complete bargains. Susan assured him he need not give himself the trouble of opening the box, as they wanted nothing of the kind. Oh ! but he only wished them just to look at them, he was so certain they would find them the *very* thing for their caps. Susan again said, in a very decided tone—

'Pray, sir, save yourself and us the trouble and time of looking over them ; we shall not become

D

purchasers, and are in haste to settle our accounts, as it is getting late.'

The man, seeing she was not to be moved by his eloquence, placed the box of 'valuables' on one side, then made out their account, which they paid, and left the shop.

'Well, Susan,' said Sally, scarcely able to restrain herself till she had got out of the shop, 'I never saw any one get away so easily, and without spending your money, too; I am certain *I* should have bought some edgings, had I been alone.'

'Then you would probably have spent three shillings, at least; so let us stop at the Savings Bank, on our way home, to add that sum to your name.'

Sally willingly complied; and I believe never afterwards laid out a shilling on an article she did not want, merely because the shopman told her it was cheap. Lucy and Cook in the meanwhile went on in their old way, encouraging each other in spending every farthing on finery, which, however, they never dared to put on, except when they went to visit their friends. They often laughed at Sally's and Susan's 'stinginess,' as they called it; but they only laughed in their turn.

CHAPTER VIII.

Preparations for the Wedding.—Unexpected delays.—
Marriage gifts of Mr. and Mrs. Harvey.

I AM, however, forgetting to tell about my favourite
James. At the end of the first year, he found
Susan had predicted too truly. The money he had
saved would only buy a chest of drawers, a bedstead, and a couple of chairs; so he went with a
heavy heart to Susan, to tell her how much he
had got, and to see if he could persuade her to get
the rest. But Susan was still '*hard-hearted*,' as
he, in a moment of vexation, called her. This,
however, did not move her.

'You know, James,' she said, 'that even if
I were willing to marry you now, my master and
mistress would not consent; for they have always
said, 'Let James furnish the house, and do *you*
keep *your* money for *future* wants; you know not
how soon they may come;' and I am sure, James,
I would not do anything contrary to their wishes.'

I have heard that James said something not
very kind about her wishing to keep all her money
for herself, but I can scarcely believe it of him;
at all events, it must have been said in a moment
of great irritation; and I am sure he would beg
her pardon the next moment, for he knew that
her proposal was for his good equally with Susan's.

D 2

After a few more conversations of a similar nature, poor James consented to wait patiently another year, and see what that would do for them; at the end of that time he found he had quite sufficient to furnish a couple of rooms most comfortably, and a small sum to spare. As the time drew near, Mr. Harvey was so kind as to allow him to see Susan twice a week instead of once, as he knew they would have a good deal to settle.

Everything seemed to be going on satisfactorily, and the wedding-day was fixed, when little Louisa Harvey was taken seriously ill; and after the doctor had said that the child's restoration, under God's blessing, would depend very much on the attention of the nurse, Susan would never leave her, except for a few hours' sleep, or to sit half an hour with poor James, who had again to bear a disappointment, (though happily not a long one;) for Susan would not leave little Louisa while she was so ill, as a change of nurse might have been attended with most serious consequences; and James was too kind-hearted and considerate to press her to do so, how much soever he migh wish it had happened otherwise.

Fortunately, little Louisa's recovery was as rapid in its progress as her illness had been, and the doctor praised Susan much for keeping the child quiet, giving her the medicine with so much regularity, and attending so strictly to her diet. At the end of six weeks, Louisa was quite herself again, and Mrs. Harvey would no longer allow

the wedding to be deferred, so on the Tuesday
following it was finally settled to take place.

Mrs. Harvey then presented Susan with a very
neat cotton gown for her wedding-dress, and a
pretty cottage straw bonnet. Little Louisa
begged to give the white ribbon to trim it, and
Miss Lizzy presented the wedding-gloves, whilst
their brothers gave her a white silk handkerchief to tie round her throat.

Mr. Harvey presented James with one of the
largest Bibles of the Society for Promoting Christian Knowledge, and it was inscribed:—

'JAMES DAWES.
From an old Master and true Friend,
Hoping that he will make it his daily companion,
and his hourly guide; that he will find it
his greatest delight in prosperity,
and his best comfort in adversity.
May 12, 18—.'

James was much pleased when he received this
very handsome present, and ran directly to show
it to Susan. 'See, Susan,' said he, 'how kind
your master has been: he has given me this handsome Bible; is it not beautiful!'

'Indeed, it is, James; and I hope we shall learn
to value its inward beauties as well as its outward
ones: you will now be doubly bound to read a
portion of it to me daily, as you have promised
to do.'

'That I will, dear Susan; depend upon it I'll
keep my word. I sometimes fancy that you

rather *doubt* me, my Susan, you so often remind
me of my promises; but to-morrow, you know,
you have *one* more promise to make to me than I
have to you, so I shall be equal with you at last;
eh, Susan, love? Come, don't look so grave; I
was only joking a bit; you'll really make me believe that you wish there was another year or
more to elapse before *you* were called upon to
make promises: why, Susan, now you are never
crying; nay, nay, I did not mean to vex you;
come, speak to me.'

After a few more tears had trickled down,
Susan assured him that he had not vexed her,
but that she was not just then in spirits high
enough to joke.

'Now that's what I just say,' replied James;
'I know you wish to be off the wedding, after
all.'

This was too much for Susan, she sobbed outright; and the more James begged her to speak,
the less power she had to do so. When she could
speak, however, she begged him to leave her to
herself for ten minutes. He consented to do so;
and on his return found her calm and composed;
and after a little difficulty, she told him he must
not think, because she was not in such high
spirits as he was, that she was indifferent about
him. 'It is quite otherwise, I assure you, dear
James; only l do, and must, feel much at parting
with my excellent master and mistress, who have
been almost parents to me; and the thoughts of
the new duties, and the new scene of life, upon

which I am so soon to enter, must bring with them much that is solemn, and much that is anxious in feeling.'

'Well, I'm sure that you'll make the very best wife in the world; so don't wet those pretty eyes any more because you are to become Susan Dawes to-morrow instead of Susan Carter.'

Susan motioned her hand for him to say no more. She was in an excited state still, and a little thing would have upset her. On going into the nursery, she found a letter lying on the table, directed to Susan Carter; she opened it, and found it contained a five-pound note from her mistress, for her unwearied attention to little Louisa during her illness. She ran directly to her mistress, and begged her not to think of giving her anything for merely doing her duty.

'But you did more than your duty, Susan.'

'*If* I did, ma'am,' said she, 'pray let it go as a *part* of what I owe to you for your constant kindness to me.'

'That I am willing to do, Susan; but *not* unless you keep the five pounds. Put it into the Savings Bank; it will be useful some day. I know you have a nice little sum there; well, take my advice, and do not *take* out one penny till you actually want it.'

Susan thanked her mistress again and again for all she had done for her, though the words were often scarcely heard in the midst of her sobs. Her mistress very kindly sat down by her; and after telling her how sorry she was to part with her, she told her that what made her forget her own regret, was the prospect she thought Susan had of being happy. 'James has always appeared a steady and religious young man; and therefore, as he has performed all his duties in that station in which God has placed him, we have every reason to believe he will make a good husband. You have both of you used all the means in your power to prevent the miseries of poverty coming upon you, that, whatever may happen hereafter, you will have nothing to reproach yourselves with on the score of improvidence.' Thus did Susan's kind mistress endeavour to calm her agitated mind; and by the time she had done speaking of all James's good qualities, Susan's tears had ceased to flow, and she was able to converse more freely with her mistress about the arrangements for the wedding morning.

CHAPTER IX.

The Wedding.—The Marriage Service.—Its effect upon
Sally.—Rejoicings in the Village.—The Cottage and
its Furniture.—Wedding Dinner at the Rectory.—
Bounty of Mrs. Harvey.—Fine Clothes don't make
good Wives.

THE bells of B—ton church rung a merry peal on
the morning of the 16th of May, announcing to the
village that Susan had now become Mrs. Dawes.
Her master had performed the service, and was
pleased to observe the reverential manner of the
bridegroom; at the same time that his countenance
beamed with joy. Poor Susan was that morning
as white as the whitest rose, and one, too, that was
bending with the drops of a heavy shower; for her
tears fell very fast, and her hand trembled so much
when she wrote her name, that I believe, if she
were now to look back at the Register, she would
scarcely know it to be her own hand-writing.

Her brother and Sally were her only attendants
at church, and as Sally had never been at a wedding before, she could scarcely wait till she reached
the vestry, to express her amazement, how any
one could hear that solemn service with levity or
inattention. Mr. Harvey overheard her as she
made the remark to George, (the Rector's late
coachman, who had accompanied James,) and said
to her, ' It is, indeed, Sally, a matter of surprise
that such should be the case; but I grieve to say

that utter thoughtlessness is too often the characteristic of the bride and bridegroom. And is it, then, a wonder that marriages which are formed without serious thought should end in utter misery? Can those expect blessings, who not only will not ask for them themselves, but will **not so** much as say a hearty 'Amen' **when the** minister begs them of God in their behalf?'

'Indeed, Sir, it is not; but I think if every one read over that solemn service before they were married, they *must* feel the awful responsibility they were taking upon themselves.'

'Yes, Sally, and mind *you* do so,' said Mr. Harvey, smiling; for he thought George seemed very attentive to all Sally was saying.

But we must not forget the bride in our serious conversation, for which I dare say she thanks us, as it has given her time to dry her tears, and be ready to join her friends, who, I doubt not, are by this time assembled at the Rectory, to congratulate the bride and bridegroom, and to eat a good breakfast with them.

The sound of the bells had filled the churchyard with all the villagers; for a wedding in the country is a thing of importance to all the village; and Miss Betty, and Miss Martha, and all the Misses of a certain age, would lose a subject of conversation if they did not see how the bride was dressed, and how she looked. Susan, too, was so beloved, that many came hoping to be the *first* to wish her every happiness, so that she could scarcely reach

the churchyard gates, for the numbers who
pressed to meet her.

At last she did get to the Rectory, and there
she found her aunt, and several other friends.
Her mistress and the little girls and boys all came
to wish her joy, and then went away, Mrs. Harvey
having very considerately arranged to take all the
children to spend that day with a friend in the
country, thinking it would be more pleasant to
the party to be left to themselves.

After breakfast, the chief of the guests went to
their different employments till one o'clock, when
they were told a dinner would be ready for them
at the Rectory, through the kindness of Mr. and
Mrs. Harvey. James and his bride, with her
aunt, went to see the cottage which was now to
be Susan's home; and it was with some degree of
pride that James drew his new relative's attention
to the substantial bedstead and chest of drawers,
which, with some very neat chairs, stood in the
bed-room; and in the kitchen everything was so
nice, and so neatly arranged, that even Susan,
who was not disposed to be very chatty, could not
help saying, 'Does not this room look comfortable, aunt?'

Her aunt, indeed, never ceased admiring, from
the time she entered the cottage till she left it;
and as she opened the cupboard, where the crockery
was kept, her admiration of the neatness displayed
in it knew no bounds. She began to take down
the cups, and arrange them on a tea-board; for

Mrs. Harvey had settled that the party should drink tea at Susan's cottage, and with her usual thoughtfulness had sent a pound of tea and two pounds of sugar to be put in the closet with the tea-things. Susan's aunt, therefore, very soon stumbled on these parcels, and pulled them out to know their contents. Susan did not know, and James could not tell; so the only way was to untie the string, and then the mystery was soon cleared up. In another corner of the cupboard stood half-a-dozen nice tea-cakes, and a good substantial plum-cake: these were presents from the young ladies and young gentlemen of the Rectory.

After having examined everything in the cottage, Susan's aunt begged James to look at his watch, and tell them what o'clock it was. To their surprise they found it was past twelve, so that there was no time to be lost in getting to the Rectory, as dinner was to be ready at one; and she whispered to Susan that she would slip away in the afternoon, and get all things ready for tea, before the rest of the party arrived there.

A substantial piece of roast beef, and a famous plum-pudding, formed the principal part of the dinner, of which a dozen of James and Susan's friends partook. Lucy and Cook were of course present, and had thus an opportunity of indulging their foolish love of dress. Their silk gowns formed a striking contrast to Susan's and Sally's (for I should tell my readers that, by this time, Sally was very nearly as neat as Susan in her appearance); and her mistress, as a proof of her approbation of her neatness, gave her a new cotton gown for the wedding.

Cook and Lucy were sadly annoyed at finding that no such present was given to them, and still more so when their mistress told them that she did not give them one, because, as they could afford to buy silk ones, of course a cotton one would not be thought of any value, and she should therefore choose two of the neatest poor women in the village, to whom she would give a gown a-piece instead of to them. They did not receive this rebuke as they should have done, but one of them (I am not sure which) said, ' It was rather hard, after slaving for their money, that they might not spend it as they chose.'

' That,' said Mrs. Harvey, ' no one can prevent you from doing, and I only claim the same privilege for myself; and as I think the gowns will be more useful to others than to you, I do not lay out *my* money for you. I wish I could convince you both, that it is your good alone I am anxious for, when I advise you *not* to spend your wages in a kind of dress which you cannot wear in my house, which is inconsistent with your station in life, and which not only prevents your *laying by* money, but actually hinders you from buying what *are* necessaries. I have often wondered what could be the inducement to servants who had any sense, thus to waste their money. Let them dress as fine as they please, they are still but servants. Finery does not make a lady : and even if you could, by this means, deceive one or more, for how long a

time could you keep up the deception? Some, I
believe, are foolish enough to think it is the way
to get a sweetheart: it *may* be so, but of this I
am very sure, that no girl would wish to *marry*
a man who loved her merely for her fine dress.'

Mrs. Harvey here thought she had made some
impression, for the countenances of both, which
were before the very picture of sullenness, now
relaxed into a slight smile.

'You own I am right I see by that smile;
come, come, I have hopes that you will yet be
amongst the *sensible* young women, and find out
that your money may be more usefully employed
than in buying fine dress.' Mrs. Harvey said no
more, but *hoped* for the best, and on the wedding-
day, as she was not at home at dinner, she did not
see that Lucy and Cook could not withstand the
temptation to deck themselves in silk gowns, and
artificial flowers in their caps, which they had
picked out of some their mistress had thrown
away.

The dinner being over, they all drank the bride
and bridegroom's health, Mr. Harvey having given
a couple of bottles of wine for that purpose. Soon
after dinner, they all went to ramble about till
tea-time, excepting Susan's aunt, who went to
the cottage, according to her promise, where at
five o'clock, they all joined her.

The evening was spent very merrily by all but
Susan, who seemed more thoughtful than any one
else. But my readers are not to suppose that she
was *sorrowful,* for that was not the case; but she

could not help feeling very deeply at leaving such friends as Mr. and Mrs. Harvey had always been to her. A few weeks, however, restored all Susan's wonted cheerfulness, and she was very cheerful. I do not know any one who impressed me more with the idea of happiness, than she did. Whatever she did, there was a zeal and alacrity about her, which seemed as if her whole heart was in it; and yet, five minutes afterwards, you might see her at some occupation, just as busy as before.

———

CHAPTER X.

Susan's conduct after Marriage. — Industry and good
    conduct of herself and Husband.—Their first Infant.
    —Beauty of the Baptismal Service.

Soon after she married, Susan began to take in a
little plain work, and do up fine muslins for the
young ladies in the village: for she found that her
own little household concerns did not occupy her
sufficiently, and she thought that she might just
as well be doing something. 'If it only pays
the rent,' said she, 'it will be a help to James.'
    James still continued groom to the squire, on
board wages, so that he always came home to his
meals, and Susan was always desirous of having
everything comfortable for him when he came
home. It was on this account that she did not
wish to take in any large washings, because in
that case she could not help having her house in
confusion at times; and as she could take a little
without inconveniencing her husband, she thought
it best to confine herself to small things, and in
these, both in ironing and sewing, she soon found
that she had plenty of occupation; besides which,
before a year had passed, she found there was a
chance of her having more employment of her own,
and some neat little caps, and shirts, and frocks,
were soon prepared for the expected little visitor.

All these were bought with the money which she had been able to earn herself, besides laying by half-a-guinea for the doctor. The forty pounds which she had in the bank when she married remained untouched, and every month her husband added ten or fifteen shillings more to it from his weekly savings.

    length the little stranger was born, and Susan had the inexpressible delight of being a mother; and truly thankful she was when her little girl was brought to her bedside for her to look at.

At the end of a week, but not before, the young ladies were allowed by their mamma to go and see Susan's baby, she having herself been two or three times, and having cautioned both Susan and her husband against allowing the village gossips to make her room the place of chattering (or *clack*, as the country folks not unaptly term it), for I am sorry to say that it too often happens when a person is confined or dangerously ill, a number of idle women collect together under pretence of nursing the invalid, but *really* for no better purpose than to gossip: for if they did not, they would not all be there at once, suffocating the poor sufferer with heat, and stunning her with their voices; but would take it in turns to sit by the sick person, and thus, by a little quiet nursing, one by one, much good would be done to the patient: instead of which, they all come together, and all leave together; so the poor creature has either to bear the noise of all, or be entirely alone.

E

James, however, strictly obeyed Mrs. Harvey, and
kept his wife quiet; the consequence of which was,
that at the end of a week she was able to sit up,
and at the end of a fortnight was quite brisk, and
able to walk about the room and dress the baby.

James made an excellent nurse both to his wife
and child: he did not, as some husbands do, make
his wife's confinement an excuse for sitting at a
public-house.   No, every spare moment that he
had, you might be sure to find him at her bedside,
or nursing the baby by the fire.

When the little girls came from the Rectory,
they brought with them a neat little straw bonnet
for the baby, and a little white frock and cap.
These were all worn when the child was taken to
be christened, which was when it was a month
old; and when Susan went to be churched.

Susan was naturally a person of great feeling,
and this beautiful service of our church for women
after childbirth affected her very much; her own
heart overflowed with thankfulness, and responded
to every word contained in it.

As she was sitting with her husband in the
evening, she remarked to him, that the more she
attended the different services of the church, the
more grateful did she feel to Almighty God that
she had been brought up a member of it. 'What
care,' she continued, 'does she take of all her
members, at every period of their lives.   From
their earliest infancy to their last resting-place in
this world has she provided services for the edifi-

cation and comfort of all her members. How deeply affecting it was to me, and I dare say to you, my dear James, to hear our good Rector baptize our infant child. How solemnly, and yet how affectionately, did he remind us, at the opening of the service, that '*all* men are conceived and born in sin,' and that our Saviour tells us, '*none* can enter the kingdom of God except he be regenerate, and born anew of water and of the Holy Ghost.' I am sure it brought the tears to my eyes, as I looked at this darling, and heard her declared by nature unable to enter the kingdom of God.'

'True, Susan,' replied her husband, 'but how immediately afterwards did the comforting entreaty follow, that we should 'call upon God, through our Lord Jesus Christ, that he would grant to *this* child, (yes, Susan, your child and mine,) that thing which by nature she cannot have, and that she may be baptized with water and the Holy Ghost, and received into Christ's holy church, and be made a lively member of the same.' See, Susan, dear, here is the passage in the Prayer Book.'

'Yes, dear James, I remember it, and those beautiful prayers which follow it; I scarcely know which I prefer: and then comes that beautiful passage from St. Mark's Gospel, so especially comforting to a mother to hear, that children were objects of interest to our blessed Saviour; and how admirably does the exhortation which follows it apply our Redeemer's words to our own infant! What is the next prayer, James?'

E 2

'It is a thanksgiving for our own knowledge of God, and a prayer that he will bestow his Holy Spirit on *this* infant, that she may be born again, and be made an heir of everlasting salvation, through our Lord Jesus Christ: you see, through-out the service, *this* infant is the object of all the prayers. Then comes the exhortation to the godfathers and godmothers, followed by those solemn promises which they make in the name of the child: it made me think what solemn promises were upon us, Susan; for at our Con-firmation, you know, *we* made these self-same promises for ourselves.'

'True, James: and did you not feel how need-ful were the prayers which followed the promises of the godfathers and godmothers, and how solemn it sounded afterwards, to hear the very words which our Saviour delivered to his apostles for the baptism of all nations, used at the baptism of our child?'

'Yes, Susan; and to hear our child received 'into the congregation of Christ's flock;' to see her signed 'with the sign of the Cross, in token that she shall not hereafter be *ashamed* to confess Christ crucified, and manfully to fight under his banner, against sin, the world, and the devil, and to continue Christ's faithful soldier and servant unto her life's end.' Oh! Susan, how does this sentence arouse all the anxious hopes of a parent for a child, that such may be indeed the case. Then come the thanksgivings that this child 'is regenerate and grafted into the body of Christ's church,' and a further prayer, ' that the rest of her life may be according to this beginning.' Then comes the Lord's Prayer, and another thanksgiving, and the service concludes with an exhortation to the godfathers and godmothers of the child, that they may not omit their duty. You see again the characteristic of our church, the interest she takes that all her members should perform their respective duties. But you are tired, my Susan: I fear my love of the church and her services has made me forget my love of my wife, which I am sure the church does not teach me to do. Come, what is to be your supper, and I will get it ready for you, whilst you prepare for bed?'

'A little bread-and-milk, James. Look in the closet, and you will see the bread, and the milk is near it.'

James took down the loaf, and cut the bread into the basin, poured the milk upon it, and then put both in a pan on the fire.

Susan could not help saying, 'Why, dear James, you are quite a nurse to me; but come, you are my chaplain too, so whilst the milk is warming, read me the usual portion of Scripture, and let us have prayers; for James and Susan never lay down in their beds without first kneeling down, and in the words of our own liturgy, praying together. The confession in the morning and evening services, or the one in the communion service, always formed a part, with such other

prayers as James might select, but on this night
they added the thanksgiving at the end of the
baptismal service.

Prayers being ended, Susan ate her supper,
and was glad to go to rest, for she had had a
good deal of fatigue and excitement that day,
and she was not yet quite strong.

————————————

CHAPTER XI.

Continued prosperity of James and Susan Dawes.—An increasing family no cause for discontent.—The Bible an unerring guide in every situation of life.

FOR a few months Susan was unable to leave her baby to go to church, but as it grew older, and began to take food, she agreed with a neighbour (a very careful and well-disposed woman) that they should go to church alternately morning and afternoon, and the other one should remain and take care of Susan's baby and Mrs. Dawson's (for that was her name) twins, who were too young to go to church. Several of their neighbours, too, used to ask them to take charge of their children; and by this arrangement (which is one that many poor people might make among themselves in a village) many more were able to attend church than formerly. In this way, year after year passed, Susan being always busy all the week, and thankful to make the Sunday a day of rest. James kept his situation, and had his wages raised, and every month continued to put by a portion into the Savings Bank, although he had several little ones to provide for.

At the end of six years he found himself the father of two boys and two girls, and very proud both he and Susan were of them, I assure you.

It was after Susan's fourth confinement, I

think, that a neighbour happened to come in, and began to pity her for having such a large young family to provide for.

'And do you think *that* a cause for pitying me, neighbour? pray spare your compassion for those who want it. I consider every child as a special blessing, and were I to repine, even had I double the number, I should think myself the most ungrateful creature possible.'

'Ah!' replied her visitor, 'but think of all the expense and bother you will have with them; and you don't know yet how many more you may have.'

'As to the expense,' said Susan, 'I allow it will be considerable, but both James and I are able to work, and I believe, by industry, we shall manage very well; and as to the bother you speak of, I don't exactly understand you; if you mean the necessary trouble which all children require, I cannot agree with you, for what is a trouble to another person is none to a mother, and it seems to me to be a marked provision of Providence that such should be the case, and that mothers should experience such delight in all the little offices for their children, that they never think of calling it a trouble. The only *real* misery to parents, I should think, must be seeing their children grow up in evil ways, and with bad dispositions; this might, I confess, tempt me to wish I had had fewer children, to have been spared such a trial, but I cannot imagine any other.'

'Well, I'm sure,' said her companion, 'it's well

for you that you think so; it's not every poor man's wife that could reconcile herself to the prospect of a large family.'

'I have no difficulty, I assure you, in doing so; indeed, it makes me tremble when I hear people grumble at an increasing family. I may be singular in my notions, but I always fancy it to be a rebelling against God, and a complaining at having blessings bestowed, which makes me fear lest God should withhold them from those who know not their value, and are so ungrateful whilst possessing them.'

'Well, to be sure, that is a very solemn way of looking at it, but I know you have serious ways with you.'

'Why,' said Susan, 'I think my notion is not *very* unreasonable; suppose, now, that the Squire had lent you several of his fields—perhaps four— one after the other, of which you were to have all the produce as long as he thought fit; and suppose that he found you grumbled very much at the labour you had to bestow on them, do you not think he would be very likely to take the fields from you, since you *not only* did *not* thank him for the loan, but actually *grumbled* at being troubled with it !'

'Why, as you say, that would very probably be the case; but I don't think I *should* grumble at such goodness in the Squire, or forget to thank him either.'

'Oh! then you think you would be *more* thankful for an act of kindness from a fellow-creature than for that greatest of earthly blessings from God, *children*. Indeed, indeed, I fear it is the case with too many of us; we do not forget to thank our earthly benefactors for some temporal and passing good, whilst we receive *daily* blessings from our heavenly Benefactor, without even a feeling of thankfulness, and perhaps with discontent.'

'It's all very true, what you say, Mrs. Dawes, I doubt not; but you see I've not been accustomed to look quite so seriously on these matters, and I've no more time just now for chattering, so I wish you a good night.'

Susan was so accustomed to be told that she had 'serious ways,' and 'strict notions,' and was 'so very particular,' that she never felt offended at it; nor did she, on the other hand, pride herself on being better than her neighbours. She always strove to do her duty both 'in word and deed,' and great good she did with her words, for many young and thoughtless mothers she was the means of reforming, and making sensible and religious women; indeed, she was quite a blessing to the village, for old and young went to her for advice and assistance, which she was ever ready to give; and she had a straightforward manner with her, and such plain, clear reasoning, that they seldom went away from her unconvinced. Does any reader wish to know what made her reasoning so convincing? It was because the Bible was the rule of her actions, and she endeavoured to make it the rule for all those who came to her for counsel. Nothing, she would often tell them, could be right or could prosper eventually which the Bible condemned, and on which they could not conscientiously ask a blessing from the Almighty.

But I fear that my reader will be tired of hearing so much of Susan at one time, so I will defer the account of her trials and her children for another occasion, hoping, in the meantime, that this little narrative may, by God's blessing, help to make more Susans amongst our scholars, our servants, and our villagers.

LONDON:
SAVILL AND EDWARDS, PRINTERS,
CHANDOS STREET.

SUSAN CARTER,

THE ORPHAN GIRL.

Part 33.

CHAPTER I.

THE last time I wrote of Susan Carter, or rather Susan Dawes, (for I am always apt to make this mistake,) it was to relate a conversation which she had one day with a neighbour, on the blessing which she considered every child to be ; and, in performance of a promise which I then made, I am now to relate how she trained hers to become so ; for she used often to say that children, as well as other blessings, would become curses, if we neglected our duty towards them. I have also to give a short account of some of the trials which have fallen to the lot of my Susan, for trials she *has* had, as I told my readers in the first part of her history : indeed the commencement of my acquaintance with her may be said to have been *one* of her griefs, for it was on the death of her old master, Mr. Harvey, that I was presented to the living of B—ton, and went to reside in that rectory, where Susan had spent so many happy years. The late rector having been

F

an old and valued friend of mine, I had frequently
stayed with him, and in our walks together he
used occasionally to sketch out the different characters of his parishioners.   I well remember, the
first time we passed the door of James and Susan's
cottage, his saying to me, 'Ah! there live my
pattern couple ; if all my parishioners were like
them, I should have but little care or anxiety
about them : ' and then, as well as at other times,
he related to me a great deal of what I have before narrated.   He promised, more than once, to
take me with him when he paid one of his pas-
toral visits to Susan, but from some cause or other
it was delayed, and I lost the benefit of his introduction.

It is now some years ago since I first called at
Susan's door ; but the circumstances connected
with it are as fresh in my mind as if it had happened only last week.   Knowing how greatly she
had been attached to Mr. Harvey, and how deeply
both she and her husband must feel his loss, I
determined to supply his place to them, as far as
it lay in my power ; but yet, on entering her cottage for the first time, I had a certain degree of
painful feeling which I cannot describe.   I knew
the contrast poor Susan would draw between the
' Old ' Rector and the ' New ' one, the hundred
predilections which she must have for her 'old'
friend, and the many prejudices which she might
have against her ' new ' one.   I waited day after
day before I summoned up resolution to go, and
introduce myself as one who was sincerely in-

terested in her and her husband, not only as their pastor, but as the friend of him whom they had so lately lost.

Poor Susan! I can see at this moment her hurried manner, and hear the faltering tones with which she begged me to be seated, apologizing at the same time for her cottage not being quite so tidy as usual, owing to her having been out all the morning attending on her aunt, who was ill. I looked around and could see but little that needed apology. She had just finished laying a clean white cloth on the table, and had placed half-a-dozen basins on it, when I entered; and, from the odour which greeted my nose, it was not difficult to discover that a good dinner of broth was preparing on the fire.

'I am afraid I am come at an unseasonable hour, Mrs. Dawes,' said I, as soon as she had seated herself, which with some difficulty I persuaded her to do, 'but I have so often passed your door, without looking in, that I thought you might begin to think that I was not following in the steps of your late worthy pastor, but was neglecting a portion of my flock at all events. 'Why, sir,' she said, with a simplicity that almost caused a smile, 'we must not look for Mr. Harvey in every clergyman. He was one of a thousand, sir, indeed he was : it will be long before we see such a man again,—such a *friend* I never expect to have here :' and she took her apron to wipe away a tear, which I saw swelling in her eyes. 'Yes, indeed, he was a good friend to you, Susan!' 'You knew him then, sir, did you?' 'Yes, I knew him, and like all who did know him, I loved and esteemed him : many are the conversations I have had with him about you and your husband; he had a great regard for both of you, I am sure.' 'Oh, sir,' said Susan, scarcely able to speak for the tears which streamed down her cheeks, ' he had always a kind word to say to us, and I dare say of us, and more than that, sir, he was always doing us some kindness ; I wish, sir, that you knew half the good that he did here. If all the village folks had been as anxious to help themselves forward, as he was to give them help, there would be less complaining than there is amongst them. I believe, sir, there is not one here, who followed his advice, that has not a little something in the Savings Bank. You'll soon see, sir, who were the followers of our good rector, for there were three things that he always told them to do, and they were,—attending church —sending their children to school—and putting by something in the Savings Bank, or Clothing-Clubs. . He was so kind to all, sir, that none but the very thoughtless could withstand him. Then in the winter, sir, he used to have soup made in his own kitchen, and given out by my good mistress to those families where the father was out of work, (as you know, sir, quarrymen and gardeners and such like must be in the winter time,) or to those who were widows with many children ; and then in the Clothing-Club, he would add a penny or more to every shilling that we deposited,

and all from his *own* money. Oh! he was indeed
a good rector. The children in the schools all
looked up to him as to a father. He often used
to say, how regularly most of them attended to
school; but, sir, I believe many of them would
rather have had a good beating at home than a
sharp word from Mr. Harvey.' 'Well, Mrs.
Dawes,' said I, smiling, ' I fear there is but little
chance of my coming up to your late worthy
rector, but I shall be glad to supply his place as
far as I can, not only to you, but to all my parishioners: it is my duty, you know, to help you
in spiritual matters, and if I can do so besides in
your worldly concerns, it will always give me
pleasure.'

At this moment James opened the door, and
not perceiving me at first, he said, ' I fear, Susan
dear, that I am behind my time, but master sent
me to inquire after our young master, who is ill
at school, and he wanted to'—Here James
observed me, and stopping short, said, ' I beg
your pardon, sir, I suppose you are our new
clergyman. I think you are the gentleman I have
seen in church the last few Sundays, and sad it
makes me to see you there; you'll excuse my saying so, sir, but we have been so long used to see
our old master there, that it will be many a long
day before we can see his place filled by another
without a tear! The grass is not yet grown over
his grave, and it will be high and thick before we
can leave off thinking of our good rector.' ' I hope
so, indeed,' I replied, ' but I will not detain you

any longer from your dinner, but hope to hear
more of him and his doings at some future time.'

At this moment, the two eldest children, who
were girls, came running in to their dinner. Their
neatness had attracted my attention at school:
there was no dirty finery on them; their hair
was not hanging half way down their backs, nor
was it dangling in their eyes, nor put up in dirty
curl-paper or fantastic plaits. No, it was cut
short all round, neatly parted down the middle,
and gave to their faces a clean and wholesome
appearance.

I have been often surprised at the fondness of
parents for keeping the hair of their children long,
and am always at a loss to account for the reason
of it. If the practice were confined to girls of
thirteen or fourteen, one might understand the
motive; but actually in my school, at this present
time, there are little things of five, six, and seven
years of age, with their hair curling, or rather
hanging (of course *curl-papers* are soon expelled
the school) down their backs! My wife does occasionally use a pair of scissors on the head of
some very slovenly offender, but it is always at
the risk of losing the little scholar altogether, if
the mother happens to be rather a foolish one.
But what I would urge upon all mothers on this
subject is, that in the first place it is injurious to
the health of a very young girl to have long hair,
by drawing on her strength for its nourishment
which would otherwise go elsewhere; secondly,
that long hair takes *much* more trouble and time

to keep clean, which to the poor must always be
a consideration ; and, thirdly, that the children
do not look nearly so well as with their hair cut
short and combed neatly.

I am, however, digressing from my narrative,
but my readers will forgive me, as the object of
my tale being to instruct as well as to amuse, they
will excuse my turning aside sometimes to do the
former.   The eldest child ran up to her mother,
saying, ' Twelve circles, mother : ' and on Susan
saying to the younger one, ' And you, Fanny,
how many ? ' she blushed and said, ' None,
mother, but two lost.'   Her mother put a basin
on a side-table, and poor Fanny placed herself by
it to have her dinner.   I must inform my readers
what was meant by these circles, or to many it
may not be intelligible. In some schools it is the
custom for a girl's merit to be judged of by her
standing at or near the top of the class : but
this plan is, I think, liable to many objections.
In the first place, a girl who is quick may easily
get to the top of the class, and then there is
nothing more for her to gain ; whereas, the plan
which we have adopted in our schools obviates
this disadvantage, as a girl's attention is not there
shown by her being at the top of the class, but by
the number of times she has been *round* the class,
and as the class is formed like a circle, each time
that a girl goes round it, is called gaining a circle,
and she takes a tin ticket with a figure on it, to
show the number of circles she had gained.   Of
course, whilst some are gaining, others are losing

circles, and the latter are shown by the figure on
the tin ticket being reversed.

This system certainly keeps up a greater degree
of life and animation in the classes, and gives the
children more interest in what they are doing.
Though I had paid Susan a longer visit than I
had intended, I could not resist the temptation
which I felt to plead for this clean and rosy-look-
ing child. She was not above six years old
apparently, but I saw her downcast eyes, and I
fancied her little lip was quivering, and a sob
with difficulty suppressed, as she stood by the side
of her basin. ' You must let me beg for my little
friend to be restored to her place, Mrs. Dawes,'
I said, ' I think she has not lost her circles wilfully.' 'I fear, sir,' said her mother, ' that
you are mistaken, and that it is owing entirely to
her own inattention that she has been losing her
circles : look up, Fanny, was it in your catechism
or your spelling that you lost them?' 'In my
catechism, mother. I had gained several circles
in my spelling.' 'Then you see, my dear child,
who was right and who was wrong, last evening.
The state of the case was this, sir. When she
came from school yesterday afternoon, just as she
had learnt her spelling, a little girl came in here
to ask Margaret and Fanny to go and drink tea
with her. I gave them leave to go in a quarter
of an hour, when I thought the lesson for to-day's
school would be learnt. They are generally good
children, sir, and are so accustomed to do what I
tell them, that it is not my habit to watch them ;

so I went into the bed-room to prepare the things for my two little boys' bed-time, and when I returned into the kitchen, to my surprise, Fanny was gone. I asked Margaret, who was still at her lessons, where her sister was, and she told me that she believed she was gone to her little friend's, but that as she could not learn her lessons so fast, she had waited to finish them ; 'but Fanny has learnt hers, mother,' said Margaret, 'for she is quicker at getting them off than I am, you know.' 'I hope she has,' was my reply; and Margaret, having put by her books, then followed her sister to drink tea at Mrs. Dawson's. When they came home, I blamed Fanny for setting off without acquainting me, and particularly as she did so before the quarter of an hour was up ; and I told her what I feared would be the consequence to-day in class, of her having thus hurried her lessons. But Fanny was *positive*, sir, (as little girls are apt to be,) and was *quite* sure she knew them, and was *quite* certain that she could say her catechism without missing a word, and you see, sir, that she must have lost more than two circles, for she had gained some in spelling.' Fanny faltered out, 'Yes, mother, I had gained six.' Upon this ingenuousness in the child, I could not help repeating my entreaty that she might place herself and her basin at the table with the others, which was at last agreed to by her judicious mother ; and charging her never again to lose her circles from a like cause, I bade this interesting family good morning.

CHAPTER II.

EACH time that I *have* visited, and *do* visit Susan, I feel more and more convinced of the incalculable blessing which a sound religious education is to the poor. Whenever I am struck by the contrast which she forms to many of my parishioners, in the management of her children, her consideration for her husband, and the striking but unpresuming example which she is to all the villagers, I can only trace it to one source. All her thoughts, words, and actions, appear to be governed by one principle, and that one the highest of all, which teaches us, in whatever station we are, to do all to the glory of God. This seemed always uppermost in her mind. To do His will, and to bring up her children in the same path, was her constant endeavour, and in this she was joined, not thwarted, by her husband. There was one custom which I always fancy was more conducive to training them 'in the way they should go,' than any other, and that was the practice of daily family prayer. I know it is the custom to say, 'that it is all very well, and very easy for gentlefolks to have their family together for prayer, but it is quite different with working people: we have our families to provide for, and must think of that;' but I am not inclined to admit this as an excuse, because it is as much the duty of the *poor* as of the *rich*, to 'seek

first the kingdom of God and his righteousness.'
I know too that some *do* practise it, and I know
that many more *might* do so, and equally sure
am I that the effect must be beneficial.

I will tell my readers how Susan arranged,
that it might cause as little delay as possible to
James. It was his custom (as it is with many
working men) to come home to his breakfast at
eight o'clock : when he did so, there lay the large
Bible (the very one his master gave him) and the
Book of Common Prayer, ready for him on the
table. The arm-chair was by them, and then on
the opposite side sat Susan with her baby on her
knee, and the other children seated on stools
waiting for him. If they had a few minutes to
spare it was filled up by the little ones saying a
hymn. When he came to the door there was
always a scramble who should have the first kiss,
but their seats were resumed immediately. He
used generally to read in the morning one of the
Psalms for the day, and then all kneeling down
they repeated together the Confession in the
Morning Service, or the Confession in the Communion Service ; then James repeated alone the
Collect for Ash-Wednesday, and then they joined
in the Lord's Prayer ; after which, the Collect
for the preceding Sunday, with the Collects for
Grace and Peace, having been said by James, he
concluded with 'the Grace of our Lord Jesus
Christ,' &c.

James has often told me that it took up much
less time than many people imagined, and only
required a beginning. In the evening he fol-

lowed the same plan, only reading the Collects in the Evening Service instead of the Morning, and reading the Second Lesson instead of a Psalm. His children were, of course, gone to bed, but he and Susan never failed to kneel down together. He used to say that he had been so accustomed at his late rector's to be present at family prayers, that he always felt quite uncomfortable when anything occurred to prevent his being present at them in his own little cottage. 'There is such a comfort,' he would say, 'in *beginning* the day well—in feeling that we have begged for God's blessing on our labours—that we have thanked Him for His care of us during the night, and begged for His protection throughout the day; in short, sir, in knowing that we are not neglecting the one thing needful. But it was our good rector who made me think so. When I first went there, if I neglected to attend family prayers he used to send for me and inquire the reason, and you may be sure, sir, I had not often a very good one, for my poor master would never admit that *any* work was a sufficient excuse for being absent at family prayers. "How long, James, do you suppose the prayers occupy?" he once said to me. "Well, sir," I replied, "it may be about seven or eight minutes, or hardly so much." "And you could not spare that time from your work, hey, James! you had gone out with the horses to water? It was more important for them to get their water ten minutes earlier, than for you to join in asking blessings ⸱us all, and hearing God's word read? Am

I so to understand your excuse for absence?" What could I say, sir? I did *not* think so, but yet I had acted as if I did. Well, sir, I'll tell you what was the *effect* of his putting the matter in this light to me. Why, I was never afterwards absent from prayer, excepting from illness, during the whole time of my being at the rectory. If ever I felt tempted to absent myself, either to get on with my work, or to save myself the trouble of washing my face and hands, I used to think of my master's question to me, and also of one which he put to a fellow-servant of mine, who had made some paltry excuse for being absent from church; and after he had finished his apology, my master paused, as if he were considering about it, and said very gravely, "You suppose, then, John, that God will accept this excuse which you have just now made me?" "Oh, sir," he replied, "I had not thought about that, but only how to save myself from *your* displeasure." "Indeed, John!" said my master; "if your excuse to me for any neglect of your duty to God is not considered sufficient by me, who am but a man, and know not your thoughts, how can you offer it to God? and believe me, if you dare not presume to make it to Him, you have been *wilfully* sinning." I remember John and I talked over the subject a good deal afterwards; and we both agreed that, whenever we were tempted to be absent from family prayers, or public worship, we would ask ourselves this question, "Can I plead the cause of my absence as a fit excuse to God?" and if not, we would pray to God that we might not yield to the temptation. Of course, sir, illness of ourselves or family would be a fitting reason why we could not attend : but I do not think any work ought to stand in the place of family worship, nor bad roads or wet weather to prevent our offering our prayers at church ; and, as to our private prayers, why, sir, I fear there will be still less excuse for us if we neglect them for our work ; for whilst our hands are occupied on this world's business, our hearts may be busy with God on the next.' But my readers are not to suppose, because James and Susan had family prayers, that their little ones were not taught to say their own prayers and praises, for that would indeed be doing them great injustice. As soon as Susan could make them understand that there is a God, who could see them at all times, and from whom they received every blessing, she taught them to pray to Him. She tried to make them understand, as soon as possible, that, as it was God who gave them everything that was good, and could alone preserve them alive and in health, they ought to do everything to please Him. At the end of this book I will write out the prayers which she taught them when they were able to learn a short form. At first she merely taught them to pray to God to make them good children, and to take care of them, and their father and mother, and all their relations and friends.

I remember she told me once that her eldest little girl (who was not at the time four years old), on seeing her sister tease the baby, went up to her, and hugging her round the throat, said, ' Don't you know, Jane, that our Catechism says, we should be *kind* to our brothers and sisters ? ' It was ' The First Steps to the Catechism ' on the Christian Knowledge Society's list, which she had learnt ; and her mother had, doubtless, on some former occasion taught her to apply it practically to herself, and then she began to do the same to her sister.

Children are most imitative creatures, as every one must have observed who has been much with them. Whatever their elders do, it is their delight to copy ; no matter what it is, if their father or mother, or whoever they are with, does it, immediately it becomes the object of their ambition. My own little girl is very fond of sitting by my side to help me to write my sermon, and must have her Bible before her, as well as I mine : and so all parents find it ; and a most important lesson they should learn from it, namely, never to do anything which they would not wish their children to copy when they should arrive at their time of life. What a useful check would this be to many thoughtless parents, if they could but be brought to bear this in mind : for surely a drunkard or swearer does not *wish* his child to be the same ; and yet he may depend upon it, that *example* is so *much* more powerful than precept, that it is in vain for him to send his child to school to be *taught* to renounce the 'lusts of the flesh,' ' to keep holy the Sabbath-day,' and ' to do his duty to God and man,' if on his return home he hears swearing, or sees drunkenness, or thoughtlessness, and want of reverence for the word of God. As the Sunday returns, he is sent to church and school, but he sees no preparation for his father and mother to meet him at public worship, or at least only occasionally; and, when they do go, if the Lord's Supper is administered, they go without even a thought of remaining to partake of it! Oh! if parents would but reflect on the ruin which is caused by such doings, (and which none can know and feel more deeply than the clergy,) surely the love of their offspring might lead them to a change of life, which higher motives have not effected. With Susan and James's children the case was widely different. They suffered not from any contrast between the instruction they received at school and the conduct which they saw practised by their parents. At school they learnt that it was their first duty 'to love God with all their heart and soul and strength,' and to do to every one as they would have every one to do to them. At home they saw their parents making the worship of God and the reading of His word the *first* business of the day, and then they felt their father's and mother's care of them, and saw their readiness to do good to all whom it was in their power to help, and thus they *saw* how they were to *do* their duty to God and man. There was no tittle-tattling or busybody-ing allowed in Susan's cottage; indeed, if any idle story was afloat, which was well substantiated, it became quite a phrase of the villagers to say, ' Well, I suppose even Susan Dawes would believe this.' She never permitted the children to bring home any tales of misconduct about their school-fellows. Anything good that they had done she was pleased to listen to, but to anything else she gave a very short reply ; and it has caused both Margaret and Fanny to have such a dislike to gossip, that no one thinks of troubling them with their chit-chat ; for, as these tattlers sneeringly say, ' they are too good to believe anything bad;' and a great recommendation it is to their mis-tresses (for they are servants now), that when they are out with the children, or sent on an errand, no time is lost in idle talking. There was another point, too, on which James and Susan were very strict, and what some of their neighbours called ' bigoted,' but it was bigotry of a kind that never hurt anybody, but would do many of us a great deal of good if we possessed it ; and this was a scrupulous attendance at their parish church. No great preacher, no travelling missionary, no farewell sermon, no school exhi-bitions, would tempt them even for one Sunday to lend their countenance to schism. James would argue thus : ' If it is wrong for me to leave the church for the meeting-house at all, it must be wrong to do so for one Sunday, for I have never yet been able to find out in other things, that doing wrong only a few times makes it less sinful at the time, though it is more than probable that if we have *once* yielded to a temptation, we shall not stop there, but go on repeating it till we know not where to stop.' This is allowed to be the case in most sins, and certainly daily expe-

G

rience shows us that it is the case with those who
yield to the temptation which 'itching ears'
offer.   Once let us leave the church to gratify
a love of novelty, or from any other motive, and
who will dare to say, that, having in so doing
resisted the Holy Spirit, we shall ever again be
permitted to join that church which we believe to
have the promise of being guided into all truth ?

James used often to tell me of several conversations which he had had with his neighbours,
and appeal to me for information, if ever he felt
himself at a loss.   The first time he seriously
discussed the matter after my coming to B—ton,
was with a Methodist one Sunday evening.   This
man had called in to tell James of a great preacher
who was to hold forth that evening; and though
he knew that James had no fancy for the Methodists, yet he thought for once, perhaps, he
might persuade him to go, as the preacher had
come from a great distance, and was collecting
money for the missionaries, and would not be
here the next Sunday.   He went on rehearsing
all this man's wonderful powers of praying extempore, and preaching extempore—his talent
for this, that, and the other, without giving James
an opportunity of replying; but when he *did*
leave off with the question, ' You'll come this
once, won't you, James ? ' put in the most per-
suasive manner, James answered with great
firmness, ' No, Simpson, thank you, I fancy I am
better employed at home.'   ' Better employed !
better employed ! ' rejoined the Methodist, opening his eyes with astonishment; ' what do you

mean? Can you be better employed than in hearing a man of piety expound the Lord's word?' 'As to his being a man of piety,' replied James, 'since he is a stranger here, as you have just told me, it would be difficult for you to know whether he is so or not; but admitting that he is, I have a notion that my time is spent more profitably at home on a Sunday evening than anywhere else.' 'Oh, indeed: then do you mean to say, that if your own parish church, of which you are so fond, was open for service, you would not go *there* on a Sunday evening?' 'I do, indeed, neighbour; I attend public worship there twice a day on Sunday, and the evening I always devote to hearing my children read the Bible and say their Catechism, for it is the only evening that I can be sure of being with them, as they are generally gone to bed when I come home on other nights; and I like to make them feel the difference between the evening of Sunday and those of the working days. Our late good rector used to say, that the evening service of his church was intended for those who could not possibly come to the other services, and that he was always sorry to see heads of families there, who, he knew, had left their children entirely neglected at home.' 'Well, that may be well enough in a general way,' said Simpson, 'but I think one of yours was just finishing her Catechism as I came in; surely you can come this *one* night: I won't ask you again—the next one is old enough to come with us, and your wife will mind the little ones.'

'My good friend,' said James, 'even if I could
be comfortable to leave my wife and little ones,
(which I confess I could not,) and take the elder
ones with me, let me tell you I could not go to
a Methodist meeting without being guilty of
gross inconsistency.' Simpson now stared more
than ever, again repeating James's words,
'Gross inconsistency! gross inconsistency! to
hear prayers from the heart, and a sermon without a book or note, or any such worldly help.'
Poor James told me he with difficulty suppressed
a smile, as he said, 'Yes, Simpson, I do think
that in going with you to hear 'prayer from the
heart,' as you call it, and 'a sermon without
note or book,' I should be acting very inconsistently: and if you have patience to hear me, I
will tell you on what authority I think so.'
Simpson pulled out his watch. 'I 've stayed too
long talking to you as it is. Mr. Wilkinson
will have begun the first prayer already; but
I 'll look in as I come back, and finish, for I
must try and get you into our meeting, even if
it be but once.' James laughed, saying, 'That
will be a harder task than perhaps you fancy;
but good-bye for the present; you can look in
as you come back, if Mr. Wilkinson does not
keep you till we are all in bed.'

Simpson then set off at full speed to hear the
great stranger. I say to hear him, for as to going to the meeting for the purpose, and with the
intention of worshipping God, that never seemed
to enter his head.

Mr. Wilkinson's prayer, and Mr. Wilkinson's sermon, seemed all he thought of. But is it *only* amongst sectarians that this spirit now prevails? Alas! how many are there amongst those who *call* themselves church people, who exhibit this besetting sin of dissenters! How many amongst us are there who will leave one church and go to another, because this clergyman has a better delivery, or that one is more pleasing, or a third is more impressive! Believe me, my readers, it is a dangerous experiment; for he who begins by roving from church to church, most frequently ends by going to no place at all, for since it is his 'itching ears' which must be pleased, he goes from one to another, seeking for novelty, and having at length *tried* all, and been *tired* by all, he thinks he can read better sermons at home, (if he feels disposed to do so,) and having never thought of going to church for the purpose of prayer, it is not surprising that he does not feel the want of it.

After Simpson had left them, Susan could not help telling James how pleased she was that he had not gone with him; 'for,' said she, 'it is now ten years that we have spent our Sunday evenings together, and I should not have liked you to have broken the *charm*—if I am not wrong in using that word: for there is a charm in the quietness of our Sunday evening, which I suspect they will not meet with in all Mr. Wilkinson's discourse; but go, my dear Margaret, and bring your Psalm to your father."

It was the custom of both Margaret and Fanny to learn a verse of a Psalm daily, and then on the Sunday evening they repeated the seven verses to their father, together with their Catechism. They both said their lessons remarkably well that evening, and even little Tommy had a hymn to say, so that James was more than ordinarily pleased at his employment. On going to bed afterwards, it was always the custom for the children to say their prayers to him instead of their mother, as he was absent during the week at their bed-time.

It was a pleasing sight (I happened once to witness it, having been sent for to baptize a child who was ill near their house, and I called in to inquire which house it was) to see him surrounded by his four children. The youngest was kneeling by his side: the three others were seated with their backs to me; his wife was sitting by the fire with her baby nearly asleep on her lap, and I motioned with my hand for him not to disturb them. Each in turn went and knelt by him, 'and soft, and sweet, and solemn, then, were the words which they did say.' I can see him now patting their little heads as they came up to him, and saying, 'Now, think, my dear child, of *all* your faults, and pray to God from your heart to forgive you.' One of them, I remember (I think it was Tommy), said in a whisper, 'I will sit still next Sunday at church, father, if God will forgive me this time.'

But I must not forget Mr. Simpson. The

prayers were heard and the children were all in bed. James had finished reading a chapter in the Bible, and the meditations for the Lord's Day in Wilson's *Sacra Privata*, when, as Susan was placing the bread and cheese on the table, there was a tap at the door, and a sound of voices. It was Simpson, and with him John Lawson.

'Here,' said Simpson, 'I have stepped in according to my promise, and have just brought Lawson with me, to show you that there are some people in the world a little more liberal than you are. Why now, he generally goes to the Independent meeting-house, yet he is *quite* willing to go to our place, or any other, when there is anything going on.' 'Oh! I can believe that very readily,' said James, laughing; 'it is the *newest* comer with all of you, I believe, who is the most welcome; and the old ones may pray and preach in the mean while to empty benches; and as, in going to the show of wild beasts which was here lately, the one (I think it was the hyena) that came from the greatest distance was considered the most curious; so the preacher who has travelled the greatest number of miles will be the most to your fancy. I am quite of another mind, and like best to meet with old friends, not only in my minister but my prayers.' 'Well,' said Simpson, 'our tastes do differ as you say, for we do like a travelling minister, for they 've so much to tell of what they 've done here and seen there—how much money they got in this place and t'other, and how they were received in this town and that, and what hardships they met with. Why, do you know, Mr. Wilkinson told us this evening, that he had worn out six pairs of shoes in walking from one to another, since he set out this time on his journeyings?' 'Oh! then,' said James, 'after all it turns out that his mode of expounding the Lord's word is by preaching about *himself*: this accounts very easily for his keeping you so long. If you had been ten minutes later, you would have got no admittance here, I can tell you, for after supper our door is closed for the night; but come, draw to the table, and take a crust of bread with us.'

'You seem to forget the purpose of our visit,' said Simpson; 'but, however, while you are telling me of the gross inconsistency of which you were saying you would have been guilty in going with me to hear Mr. Wilkinson, I'll employ myself as you desire; so now I'll thank you for a plain answer to a plain question, "Pray, what makes it so inconsistent?"' 'Before I answer your question,' said James, 'you must allow me to put one to you.' 'With all my heart,' said Simpson. 'Well then,' said James, 'would you not think it strange in any friend of yours, who you knew had been praying in the morning at church against any known sin, and begging of God to keep him from it, (suppose, by way of example, that it was drunkenness,) to stop as he came from church at the first public-house on his

road, and sit drinking there till perhaps he could not walk home by himself? I ask you, whether you would not be apt to say that the prayer of that man was a mockery? and might we not expect to see almost *immediate* punishment follow so wilful a despising of God's known commands?'
'Indeed I should; but I don't exactly see what drunkenness has to do with going to hear Mr. Wilkinson.' 'Perhaps not,' said James; 'but it is possible that I may be able to show you a passage in the Litany, which *has* something to do with going to hear Mr. Wilkinson. I believe you have sometimes been to church, but probably you do not remember to what I allude, so I will fetch the Prayer-book and show it to you; see, this is the petition:—' From all false doctrine, heresy, and schism, from hardness of heart, and contempt of thy word and commandment, *Good Lord deliver us!*' Now, I consider that having this morning joined earnestly in this prayer, I should act almost, if not quite, as inconsistently in going to the meeting-house in the evening, as a person who had prayed against drunkenness would do in spending the day at a public-house. You look surprised, Simpson, but in doing so, I should undoubtedly have been guilty of *schism.* I might very possibly have heard both *false doctrine* and *heresy,* and in forsaking the church I should have shown *hardness of heart, and contempt of God's word and commandments.*' 'But let us understand each other,' said Simpson: 'first of all tell me what you mean by *schism?*'

' By schism I mean separating from the church.'
' Well, and so do I; but there's many a Methodist
who yet belongs to the Church.' ' You will
excuse me, Simpson, if I say, that he who attends
church and meeting, is "halting between two
opinions;" he is, as it were, trying to serve God
and please his own " itching ears " at the same
time, by going in the morning to hear the minister
ordained of God, and in the evening the minister
set up by man.' ' How so?' said Simpson;
' what right have *you* to make this distinction?
why may not our ministers be as much ordained
of God as yours?' ' Again, I must answer your
question by putting another to you : do you think
if God has made known the way in which it is
most acceptable to Him that we should ask for
a blessing, that we have a right to choose some
other way more agreeable to our fancies?' ' Indeed, I think we have not; but I am not aware
that He has given us any commands about ordaining ministers ; but I see we shall not end our
debate to-night, and it is getting late, so I must
bid you good-bye, and look in during the week.'
' Do so,' said James, ' and I will look out some
texts of Scripture in the mean time, to prove to
you that the ordination of our ministers is according to the example and instruction of the
apostles, who you know were inspired, and one of
whose injunctions it was, " Let all things be done
decently and *in order*." '

CHAPTER III.

In a few days after this conversation, Simpson called again. 'Well, James,' said he, 'here I am come back to the battle; you see I am not afraid of being made a churchman by you.' 'I hope you are not *afraid*, Simpson, indeed,' said James, 'for if I could prove to you that the Church is supported by Scripture, and that dissent is condemned by it, I hope that you will no longer play the truant; for, after all, I must think that such is your case. You were, I believe, baptized in the Church, confirmed in the Church; your children are all of them taken there to be baptized, and thus become members of the Church —some of them are buried there, and by the side of them, some day, (and you know not how soon,) you will, probably, be laid: and yet, for the last three years, have you forsaken her ministrations, and have so far forgotten your mother, that you cease to call yourself by her name: for though you say that many a Methodist belongs to the Church I suspect *you* would not be pleased at being called a Churchman: indeed, I scarcely know by what name you ought to be distinguished, as I believe, in the last six weeks, you have attended three different meeting-houses.' 'Why, I am a Methodist nominally, but I don't object to go and hear any one who I think may do me good, whether he be Methodist, Baptist, or Independent.' 'And it has never struck you,' said James, 'that there was any harm in so doing?' 'Quite the reverse, I assure you: where I think I get the most good, there I think I ought to go.' 'And you have found great benefit to yourself, have you, Simpson, in hearing these strange preachers?' 'Why, certainly, I *have* felt edified by them.' 'You surprise me: what, by knowing how many pairs of shoes they wear out: that *must* be edifying!' 'Come, come, James, none of your jesting!' 'Well, excuse me this once, but it came into my head just then, how strange it would have been had the rector 'expounded the Lord's word,' as you express it, in such a manner—however, let us hear the *result* of these edifying preachers: tell me now, candidly, (for I am willing to answer any like question which you may afterwards put to me,) have their prayings and preachings helped you to conquer one *known sin*, or assisted you to frame your mind more generally for prayer and meditation—in short, do you find yourself serving God more earnestly than when you attended the church?' 'You are coming to close quarters now, James, but, perhaps, I shall make you pay for it, when it is my turn to catechise you; however, I must confess, that my feelings *out* of the meeting-house, are very unlike those which I have when I am in it. I am often excited there, but unluckily, the excitement goes off as I leave the minister who produced it. Our

preachers certainly have the knack of stirring up
our feelings, but, somehow or other, the fire goes
out between whiles, and has to be fresh-lighted
by every preacher.' ' Oh ! Simpson, if you confess such to be the case, I *have* hopes that you
are not quite irrecoverably lost to us, so let me
at once show you a few of the texts which will
prove to you the sinfulness of schism, and do
promise me that you will look fully into this
matter, and with an earnest desire to find out
the truth.' ' Why, certainly,' said Simpson,
' I should like to know that I was in the right,
but I have many objections to the Church, which
you must first let me tell you of.' ' No, no,'
said James, ' I claim the privilege of being
spokesman first, as I have myself to defend, for
refusing your request to accompany you to hear
that great gun of a preacher; and besides, I fancy
that if I can prove to you that you are wrong in
going to dissenting meeting-houses, your objections will very quickly be answered afterwards.' James then went to the shelf, and
brought down the Bible, and in it was the slip
of paper on which Mr. Harvey had marked
down a few of the passages in Scripture, to prove
to James that schisms or divisions (for the words
have the same meaning) are condemned by the
apostles.

The first place was from 1 Cor. chap. i. ver.
10 : ' Now I beseech you, brethren, by the name
of our Lord Jesus Christ, that ye all speak the
same thing, and that there be no divisions among

you.' The next was from 1 Cor. chap. xi. ver. 17—19 : ' Now in this that I declare unto you, I praise you not, that ye come together, not for the better, but for the worse. For first of all, when ye come together in the church, I hear that there be divisions among you, and I partly believe it, for there must be also heresies among you, that they which are approved may be made manifest among you.' The next passage is a very striking one, it is from Romans, chap. xvi. ver. 17 : ' Now, I beseech you, brethren, mark them which cause divisions and offences, contrary to the doctrine which ye have learned, and avoid them.' In the 4th chapter of Ephesians, 3, 4, 5, and 6 verses, St. Paul says, ' Endeavouring to keep the unity of the spirit, in the bond of peace. There is one body, and one spirit, even as ye are called in one hope of your calling, one Lord, one faith, one baptism, one God and Father of all.' Thus as far as the apostle's words go, it is as false and unchristian to make more *bodies* than one, as to have more Lords than one, more Gods than one, more creeds than one. After reading these texts, James said, ' Now I wish to know how it is possible for any one to fall into this sin, if Dissenters are clear of it ? What *is* the sin, if separation from the existing church is not ? This is my poor master's comment, you see, Simpson, on that verse, but I think he told me that he copied it from the writings of some good man who lived soon after the apostles, but I forget his name.'

' Well, go on,' said Simpson, somewhat snap-pishly, ' or we shall not get through to-night.'

' The next text which is marked down, Simpson, is but too applicable to the present time: it is from St. Paul's Second Epistle to Timothy, in which there is so much to be learned about the duties of all the members of the Church. The passage is in chap. iv. ver. 3, 4 : " For the time will come that they will not endure sound doctrine, but after their own lusts will they heap to themselves teachers, having itching ears, and they shall be turned unto fables: " and the next text is from the Second Thessalonians, chap. iii. ver. 6 : " Now we command you, brethren, in the name of our Lord Jesus Christ, that ye withdraw yourselves from every brother that walketh disorderly, and not after the tradition which he received of us." To the Hebrews, chap. viii. and at the 8th and 9th verses, the same apostle says, " Jesus Christ, the same yesterday, and to-day, and for ever. Be not carried about with divers and strange doctrines." I remember our good rector saying, that this meant that as *Christ* was the same always, so was his doctrine. The other verses are from the other Apostles, showing that divisions even thus early had crept into their different congregations. St. Peter says in his Second Epistle, chap. ii. ver. 1, 2, " But there were false prophets in those days, even as there shall be false teachers among you, who privily shall bring in damnable heresies, even denying the Lord that bought them, and bring upon

themselves swift destruction.   And many shall
follow their pernicious ways, by reason of whom
the way of truth shall be evil spoken of."   St.
John says in his First Epistle, chap. iv. ver. 1,
" Beloved, believe not every spirit, but try the
spirits whether they are of God : because many
false prophets are gone out into the world." The
concluding text on my list is from St. Jude, and
very emphatic it is. " Beloved, remember ye the
words which were spoken before of the Apostles
of our Lord Jesus Christ.   How that they told
you there should be mockers in the last times, who
should walk after their own ungodly lusts. *These
be they who separate themselves*, sensual, having
not the Spirit."   Now then, Simpson, I have
stated the *first* part of my charge against you,
and all other schismatics, and that is that you *do*
" separate yourselves."   Now what have you to
say in reply ? '

'Why, first let me cast my eye over the texts
again.'

'Well, here is the beginning of those I have
read.   In the first two "*divisions*" (or schisms,
for in the margin of the Bible it is the latter
word) are condemned by St. Paul ; so let us
hear how it is that you can approve and follow
what he condemned.'

'Why, in the first place, I did not make the
division, and, in the second, I don't consider that
I have *altogether* left the *Church*, though I am a
Methodist, for our founder, John Wesley, was a
churchman.'

'I fear, Simpson, in the last day, it will be
considered *no* excuse for doing evil, that others
had set us the example.   Eve set Adam the
example of·eating the forbidden fruit, but Adam
was, notwithstanding, turned out of the garden,
and became subject to sin and death, the same as
Eve.   His excuse of the "*woman*" having given
it to him, and hers of the "*serpent*" having "be-
guiled" her, were alike rejected by God: and so
it will be with us, Simpson; whether the world,
or the devil, tempts us, it will not be accepted by
our Maker: and as to your being still of the
Church, I must answer you in the words of St.
John: "They went out from us, but they were *not*
of us: for if they had been of us, they would no
doubt have continued with us: but they went
out, that they might be made manifest, that they
were *not* all of us."   John Wesley indeed *began*
by being a churchman, but he *ended* by being a
schismatic.   He began by wishing to make services independent of the Church—he ended by
forsaking the services of the Church altogether.
It is useless for you to say that you are "of the
Church," or "friendly to the Church," as so many
of you do; for if you were so in reality, why
not belong to her altogether? Why not build
churches *instead* of meeting-houses? I fear,
indeed, one of the causes of Methodism was a
love of ease: (I will tell you afterwards what
followed from this love of ease.) It was *easier* to
build a meeting-house—it cost less money to do
so; and to supply the preachers on John Wesley's
H

plan was still easier ; and therefore, in order to get a few more services in places, which, I admit, often were in want of them, with as little trouble and expense as possible, the Apostle's injunction was forgotten, of keeping the unity of the spirit in the bond of peace.

' No one, I dare say, doubts the good *intentions* of John Wesley : no one can deny his zeal, but, as churchmen, we must regret his want of judgment, and (to call it by no harsher name) his utter forgetfulness of the solemn vows which he made when he was ordained deacon and priest. I have often wondered how a man, who thought so much upon religion, could reconcile it to his conscience.'

' But,' said Simpson, ' how do *you* know what vows he made when he was ordained ? '

' How do I know ? ' said James, ' why, by my Prayer-book, to be sure. Have you never read the Services for the Consecration of Bishops, and Ordering of Priests and Deacons ? '

' Not I, indeed, I did not so much as know that there was a service for that purpose. If a man can make a good prayer, and preach a sermon without having to look on a book the whole time, as your fine church-ministers do, that 's enough for me: it 's a pretty good proof that the man has had " a call," and that's more, I suspect, than many of your ministers can say.'

' Oh ! Simpson, how can you say so ? Are you then ignorant that it is the *want* of the " call " to preach that we complain of in your sect and in

all others ? But let me show you our services
for " calling," or setting apart, our ministers.
You will not have time to read all over now, but
see in the Service for the Ordering of Priests,
(and there is a similar one in that of Deacons ;)
John Wesley was asked this question by the
Bishop : " Will you then give your faithful dili-
gence always so to minister the doctrine, and
sacraments, and the *discipline* of Christ, as the
Lord hath commanded, and as this Church and
realm hath received the same, according to the
commandments of God ; so that you may teach
the people committed to your care and charge to
keep and observe the same ? " To which Wesley
must have replied, " I will do so, the Lord being
my helper." Now, I ask you as a fair man, did
he keep this solemn promise ? Did he not lose
sight of all church discipline ? Did he not act
directly contrary to it, in preaching in meeting-
houses, and this too at a time when he was pro-
fessing attachment to the Church ? Did he not
further do so in using extempore prayer ? And
—not to mention other smaller things—did he
not take to himself the right of ordaining ministers ? Indeed, I have heard that he pretended
even to consecrate bishops ; but it seems too ab-
surd to suppose a priest could make a bishop ;
one might as readily imagine that you or I could
make a duke of neighbour Lawson: but if it was
so, it only proves that when once Satan tempts
us to go out of the right path, with the seducing
words, " ye shall be as gods,"—which is too often

the bait he holds out to separatists,—he does so
entirely blind the eyes of his followers, that they
presume to act as such.'

'Oh, then,' said Simpson, 'you do mean to
say that your bishops of the church are as gods,
do you ?'

'This question I can answer better in St.
Paul's words than in any of my own. Perhaps
you may remember the passage where he says,
"Now then we are ambassadors for Christ, as
though God did beseech you by us, we pray you,
in Christ's stead, be ye reconciled to God." I
think nothing can be plainer than this.'

'And do you really mean to say that you do
not think Methodist ministers, and Independent
ministers, and many others, are just as much ambassadors for Christ, as your church ministers ?'

'I cannot for one moment suppose that they
are.'

'And why not, pray ? I am sure that many
of them are every bit as good men as any of your
ministers—aye, just as good as your great favourite, Mr. Harvey.'

'As to that, Simpson, it has nothing at all to
do with the matter, even if we could decide on
their goodness ; which, however, as we are but
erring men, and cannot see into their hearts, we
are not able to do. All that I maintain is, that
if we refuse to use the means which God appoints
for obtaining a blessing, we have no right to expect it on means of our own selecting ; and if we
choose to set up altar against altar, and one says,

I am of Paul, and another, I of Apollos, and a third, I am of John Wesley; Christ is divided, and it is clear that we are not all " one," as our Saviour prayed that His disciples might be, and that *one* Spirit is not guiding the actions of all.'

' Well, but after all, if the Church is right, it seems very odd that there should be so many who dissent from her.'

' Is it, indeed ?   You think, then, that we are all naturally prone to the right way, do you ? You find it so with yourself, Mr. Simpson ? And the Jews who heard our Saviour's discourses, they *all* followed him, did they not ? '

' Come, come, James, none of your jesting, for I see your drift.'

' I am glad you do, for if your argument was correct, our Saviour and His Apostles would have had the greatest number of followers, and there would have been no schisms then ; whereas you know, in every Epistle of the Apostles, there is some reference to them, and many injunctions given to the different churches for their guidance ; and I think you will not find that self-appointed ministers are according to their directions. Does not St. Paul say, in reference to this subject, " No man taketh this honour to himself, but he that is called of God, as was Aaron. So also Christ glorified not himself to be made a High-priest, but he that said unto him, Thou art my Son, this day have I begotten Thee." '

' Well,' said Simpson, ' this verse never struck me before ; but I don't see, as I said just now, that our ministers are not just as much "called of God," as yours.'

'Why, my dear fellow, how do you make that out, when our ministers are ordained in the way which Christ appointed by His Apostles, and yours are not?'

'Pray, prove that to me, for I am a little unbelieving.'

'I must again begin by asking you a few questions, Simpson, that we may be certain we understand one another. First, then, when our Saviour ascended into heaven, and His Apostles were on earth, do you think that what they said and did was by the direction of the Holy Spirit?'

'Why, I should think there can be no doubt of that.'

'Very well, so far we are agreed; the next point is, do you think that what they wrote concerns us at all?'

'Certainly I do.'

'And perhaps you will also agree with me, that it is *probable* their manner of appointing ministers would be the *right* one?'

'Why, considering that the Holy Ghost was their guide, I suppose one could not very well deny that.'

'And, if I can prove to you that dissenters do *not* follow the example of the Apostles in the appointment of their ministers, and that the Church follows closely in the Apostles' steps, perhaps you will agree with me in thinking this a strong argument against dissent in *all* its forms; for there is not any kind of schism which bears this mark of a *true* church, excepting the Church of Rome.'

'By the bye, your speaking of the Church of Rome, reminds me that, if Methodists, Independents, Baptists, and others, are dissenters from your Church, you are dissenters from the Church of Rome.'

'I believe you are again wrong there; but before touching upon that subject, which I will do presently, let me proceed to show you what foundation the Church has for the setting apart of her ministers. I will do so as shortly as possible, as there are other points which we must talk over before I can look forward to your being a member of the Church once more.'

'I think we had better wait till to-morrow night,' said Simpson, 'for it is now half-past nine, and I will come as soon as I get myself cleaned after my work.'

'Do so,' said James, 'and we will consider this subject seriously, for it is an important one.'

CHAPTER IV.

BEFORE the clock struck seven, and before James had finished his tea, Simpson was at the door. 'Come in, come in,' said James, as he saw Simpson inclined to withdraw, when he perceived that James was at tea, 'I am ready for you·; but perhaps you will take a cup of tea first, to brace you up for the battle.' Simpson declined, saying that he had already had some, but begged James not to hurry himself, as they had a long evening before them. 'It will not be *too* long, I warrant you,' said James, 'so let us at once proceed to business. It is the formation of the ministry that we have first to consider. In the Church, as you know, the ministry is composed of three orders—Bishops, Priests, and Deacons; and the reason of this is, that these three orders are distinctly marked out in the Epistles of the Apostles. If you turn to 1 Tim. chap. iii. eighth and following verses, you will see St. Paul gives directions to Timothy about the ordination of deacons, which shows that he was superior to them. The words are, " Likewise must the deacons be grave, not double-tongued, not given to much wine, not greedy of filthy lucre; holding the mystery of the faith in a pure conscience." You can read the other verses at your leisure. In St. Paul's Epistle to Titus, chap. i. ver. 5, he says, " For this cause left I thee in Crete, that thou shouldest set in order the things that are wanting, and ordain elders in every city, as I had appointed thee." Now, " Elder," in the Greek language, in which, you know, the New Testament was written, is called " Presbyter," and this has been shortened into " priest ; " so you see these two orders are plainly spoken of by St. Paul ; and he gave Timothy and Titus power to ordain both, so that both Timothy and Titus must have been superior to priests and deacons. In the Apostles' times the priests were often called " *bishops*," as well as Presbyters, as you will see in the 1st Timothy, chap. iii.'

'Why, James, where did you get all this learning?'

'Why, a good deal of it I got by reading some of the tracts which my poor master gave me. They are all on this list of the Society for Promoting Christian Knowledge. Here is one which I will lend you ; it is *On the Authority of a Threefold Ministry*. But I will be candid, and tell you that our rector has been brushing me up a little for my argument with you, for I told him the other day what we had been talking of, and what we had yet to speak of ; and he told me I must explain to you the reason why "priests" were called "bishops" in the Apostles' days. It was this :—The word "bishop" means overseer ; now the priests are overseers to their *flocks*, and the bishops are overseers to the priests and deacons. You must recollect that the *Apostles* were then in the place of our bishops, that they held the *first* office in the Church, and they were sometimes called "Apostles," sometimes "messengers," and sometimes "angels," for angel and messenger have the same meaning. If you will wait a minute whilst I go to my drawer, I will show you it all very clearly put down by our rector the other day, when he was here ; he copied it out of a little tract called *The old Paths, where is the good Way?* which he had in his pocket, but which he said he could not give me then, as he had not another of them. You know what I am now proving to you is, that there were three orders in the first formation of the Christian Ministry, just as there had before been three orders in the Jewish priesthood.'

James then went for the paper, and began reading the following passage :—

'During our Lord's stay on earth, He was the Great High Priest. He alone had an inherent right to act in this capacity. He alone could offer sacrifices for sin, and make reconciliation for man. He alone had power to grant a commission. All others are merely His humble representatives, acting in his name, and by His authority. This our great *High Priest* had under Him twelve *Apostles*, and seventy *disciples*. During the Apostles' days, the highest order consisted of the *Apostles ;* the second order was called bishops, elders, or presbyters, and the third, of those styled deacons. From the Apostles' time to the present, the high order has been named bishops, archbishops, and patriarchs ; the second order has been denominated presbyters, priests, or elders ; and the third has always been named deacons. But it is not by *names* but by *offices* that the orders of Christian priesthood are best distinguished. A name is nothing : it is the authority and office which distinguish the order : even before the Christian era, the church of God was distinguished by a *three-fold order of priesthood*, and so, as a shadow, exhibited exactly what we now see in substance.'

'Now, Simpson, what do you say to that?'

'Why, that I must go home, for I have had a long enough lesson for one evening.'

'Nay, nay,' said James, 'you are never tired yet; why, you have scarcely been here an hour.'

'You forget, James, that all you have been saying is *new* to me, and I shall require some time to think it all over, before I quite understand it.'

'Well, you are right, I dare say, so I will give you this slip of paper to study by yourself. Take care of it, for I may find it useful among some other of my dissenting acquaintances.'

CHAPTER V.

WHEN Simpson brought back the slip of paper, James asked him, if he thought *now* that there was any ground for the Church asserting the divine authority of a three-fold Ministry?

'Why, I must say,' said Simpson, 'that it seems pretty clear that there were three orders in the Apostles' times, though their names were not quite the same as they are now.' 'Yes,' said James, 'and there is one remark our minister made on this subject, which I must say, even independently of the Scriptures, ought to have *some* weight with us, and taken in connexion with them is a very powerful argument in favour of our form of church government, and it is this : that until the Reformation there never had been a church in any part of the world that was not governed by bishops, priests, and deacons ; and this was for the space of fifteen hundred years. We assert that our Church is built on the foundation of the Apostles and prophets, Jesus Christ Himself being the chief corner-stone : we love our antiquity, whereas there is not one of the dissenters who can date the existence of their sect beyond three hundred years ; and as to you, who call John Wesley your founder (which carries in itself the mark of schism), a hundred years have not elapsed since he gave birth to you.   One of our great and good bishops said that "there can nothing of more weight be said against religion than that it is new," and I think you must agree with me that he is right.   Can you for a moment suppose that the holy Apostles were *not as well* instructed as John Wesley, or Whitfield, or Knox, or Calvin, when you admit yourself that they were divinely inspired : and is it a matter of no importance whether we follow in their steps or not ?'

'But,' said Simpson, 'in things *indifferent*, I don't exactly see that it is of consequence whether we do as they did or not.'   'And who, then, is to decide which are the things that are indifferent and which are not ? *you* will think,

perhaps, that it is immaterial whether there is
one order in the Ministry ; your next neighbour
may think that it is not necessary to attend
public worship in a church at all, since he can
read and pray at home; whilst a third may think,
that the sacraments are simple ordinances, and
that it is ridiculous to attach any peculiar efficacy
to them ; so that with these three opinions, which
each would consider to be about a thing "indifferent," there would speedily be an end to the
Ministry, and, indeed, according to the two latter
opinions, there could be no necessity for one ;
and this should make us see the wisdom of God
in not leaving each of us to decide on the com-
parative merits of different parts, as I suspect we
should be inclined to consider those things "indifferent" which did not happen to suit our own
tastes and fancies.'

'Then, pray, who is to decide for us on all
these points?' 'The same kind friend, my
dear Simpson, who is always ready to give us
help, if we will but receive it. Yes, our mother
Church is a "witness, and keeper of holy writ,"
and she will not permit that anything contained
therein, having the sanction of the Apostles,
should be considered a thing indifferent: and
as I think I have proved to you that our Saviour
Himself, as well as the Apostles, appointed different orders in the Ministry, let us now proceed
to the *appointment* of these ministers.' 'Yes,
yes, that is *the* point, after all,' said Simpson,
'and I guess that you will find in the New Tes-

tament, that it is the *inward* call that is necessary to make ministers.' 'I grant you that
most fully, and if you had read the services of
the Church, you would have seen that it is the
very first question which the bishop asks of those
who come to be ordained, whether they have
this "inward call." The words are these, " Do
you trust that you are inwardly moved by the
Holy Ghost to take upon you this office and
ministration, to serve God for the promoting of
His glory, and the edifying of His people ?" and
the person answers, " I think so." The next
question is, " Do you think you are truly called,
according to the will of our Lord Jesus Christ,
and the due order of this realm, to the ministry
of the Church ? " He answers to this, " I think
so." Now surely you must admit that nothing
can assert the inward call more clearly than this;
but then the difference between dissenters and
the Church is, that *we* say an *outward* call is
also necessary, and they deny this : and what is
worse, many of them assert, most mistakenly,
(as I think I have proved to you,) that we do
not acknowledge any but an *outward* call.'

'Well, but after all, the " inward call " is the
main thing ; let a man have that, and I think
he may get on without the latter.'

'*You* think so, Simpson ; but who made *you*
a judge in that matter ? Is it to be supposed
that a man living eighteen hundred years after
our Saviour is to consider *his* opinion on a point
of church government as good as that of the

divinely inspired Apostles? Besides, what did our Lord Himself do, when He gave them the commission to go and preach to all nations? did He not breathe on them, saying, "Receive ye the Holy Ghost?"'

'Well, James, but what does this prove? Nothing more I conceive than that *they* received the Holy Ghost; and I suppose you don't mean to say that your church ministers receive it in the same manner when they are ordained.'

'Not in the same *manner*, certainly, for our Saviour is not *personally* present to confer it; but if you look at the service of the Church again, you will see that *we* do believe that the Holy Ghost is thus conferred " for the office and work of a priest in the church of God," just as the Apostles received it from our Saviour when they were ordained by Him with the very same words, " Receive ye the Holy Ghost; " for you must remember that they transmitted it to others by the laying on of their hands. Indeed, if you only study the Scriptures attentively you will see that the strongest proofs of a disciple being *able* to teach was not sufficient to make him a minister, without first being ordained by the Apostles.'

'Well, James, I see it is as you say; but after all I cannot bring myself to think that the laying on of your bishops' hands can have the same power as the laying on of the Apostles' hands had then; for when has the Holy Ghost descended on them as it did on the day of Pentecost?'

'That was to give them miraculous powers; for, as we have just observed, our Saviour first gave the Holy Ghost for the work of the ministry; and you know the Apostles ordained Matthias in the place of Judas *before* the day of Pentecost. But what is the stumbling-block in the way of your belief? Is it because our bishops are but *men*, that you are so difficult to convince?'

'Just so.'

'Then do look at this subject in another light, and consider that they are "ministers of God," and "ambassadors of Christ," and then I think you will see that God will endow them with spiritual gifts, for a spiritual work: besides, if this is not the case, those comfortable words which our Saviour addressed to the Apostles, when He gave them their commission, cannot be fulfilled. You must remember them, I am sure: "Lo! I am with you always, even to the end of the world." Surely you must admit that this could only refer to their office, for St. Peter and the Apostles died but a few years afterwards, and therefore this promise can only refer to those who hold that office in an uninterrupted succession from the Apostles.'

'I see, James, you catch me at every word; your minister has trained you well, at all events, to make out a strong case in favour of the Church;

but let me observe to you, that close as your bishops may keep to apostolic practice in one respect, they are rather different from them in another. Look at the poverty of the Apostles, and then see the riches of your bishops.'

' Oh ! you think that their having more wealth makes them less able to preach, do you ? You do not think with St. Paul, that, if we reap their spiritual things, it is not a greater matter if they reap our carnal ones. Perhaps you do not know that it was a feeling very different to that which you express towards them, that gave them their riches. Yes, Simpson, it was the piety of our forefathers which endowed the several bishoprics with the wealth that belongs to them.'

' No, indeed, James, I was not aware of that, and I suspect, if we had our way, instead of giving money to them, we should rather be inclined to take it from them, if we only knew how to manage it.'

' Why, as to that,' said James, ' if you can prove to me, that you have a right to take the squire's (my master's) lands from him, of course you would *then* (but not before) be able to find out a way to seize the money belonging to the Church. Supposing you had £5000, or £6000, left to your family, some hundred years ago, you would think it rather odd, if you heard any one planning how to get hold of your money !'

' Why, I can tell you this, they might plan as long as they liked, for they would not get it ; but I don't think any one that was not a down-

I

right swindler or robber would dream of such a thing.'

'I quite agree with you; and, when I hear people talking in that foolish way of wishing to get hold of some of the money of the bishops and clergy, I cannot help telling them that they must be very anxious to have a rope round their necks to talk so; for that they cannot have any more right to it, than to Lord John's park or horses. The only difference between the money belonging to a nobleman, or squire, and that belonging to a bishop, is, that in the case of the latter it goes to the successors in the *office*, and in the former it goes to the heirs by *birth*. But, supposing that it was possible by any means, not dishonest, to get possession of this wealth, (which, I believe, is generally fancied to be much larger than it is,) how do *you* expect to be benefited?'

'Well, I don't know that *I* might be any the better for it.'

'No, no, never fancy such a thing for a moment. We see how the clergy generally spend their money; that they give more to the poor and needy than any other class of people, and surely they have as good a right to live in comfort as the fox-hunting nobleman, or the dashing squire; and all I can say is, that, if the wealth of the clergy was doubled, I think the poor would be the gainers; for if they whose life is devoted *exclusively* to the service of God know not how to spend their money for the good of their fellow-creatures, there is but a poor chance, indeed, for those doing so who are occupied in the cares, and pleasures, and business of this world.'

'Well, now, there's a good deal of truth in what you say, I must confess. I see you have thought more on these matters than I have done, and I don't think I shall again be so ready to take other people's sayings, without considering about them; however, I have got two or three more questions for you, but not to-night, for it is late, and my wife is not over well pleased at my being so often out in an evening, though, as she knows I am in *good* company,' (said Simpson, laughing,) 'she does not make such a noise about it as she would otherwise do; so here's good night to you, and yours. I'll be back again as soon as I can get *leave*.'

CHAPTER VI.

A WHOLE week elapsed before Simpson returned, and then he said he could only stay a short time, as his wife was not well, and was not willing to lose his company; 'so we must proceed at once to business,' said he. 'Now, what I wish to observe to you is this; that, fond as you are of the Church, you will not deny that there are *some* bad men amongst your ministers; and, if your

rector was so, would you not then think that you
had a just reason to leave the Church, for a time
at all events?'

'Here, again, Simpson, you are all wrong.
You forget what a Church is.   Can you suppose
that it is the personal holiness of the minister
which makes our worship acceptable to God?
You shall see the Article of the Church, however,
on the subject; for I do like to show you, that
there is scarcely any question of this sort which
you can ask me that I cannot answer in the
words of the Church.   See, it is the Twenty-sixth
Article.

' " Although in the visible church the evil be
ever mingled with the good, and sometimes the
evil have chief authority in the ministration of
the Word and Sacraments, yet forasmuch as
they do not the same in *their own name, but in
Christ's*, and do minister by His commission and
authority, we may use their ministry, both in
hearing the Word of God and in receiving of the
Sacraments.   Neither is the effect of Christ's
Ordinance taken away by their wickedness, nor
the grace of God's gifts diminished from such as
by faith and rightly do receive the Sacraments
ministered unto them; which be effectual because
of *Christ's institution and promise*, although they
be ministered by evil men."

'The doctrine of our Church is plainly stated,
so I have nothing to do but to prove its truth by
Scripture.   Our minister preached a Sermon last
Sunday on this very subject, and I could not help

thinking at the time that he intended it as a
help to me in my argument with you.

'His text was from Jeremiah, chap. xvii. v. 5.
—" Thus saith the Lord, Cursed be the man that
trusteth in man, and maketh flesh his arm, and
whose heart departeth from the Lord ; " and he
explained the very Article which we have just
been looking at, and proved its truth by several
examples taken from Scripture, which I will give
you as well as I can remember. After saying
that the office did not *derive* its holiness from
the man, and therefore that their wickedness
could not make it sinful ; and that as the sacraments are still holy, though administered by sinful
men ; he gave the reason of it in the words of
the Article :—" Because they do not the same in
their own name, but in Christ's." The ordinances
are Christ's—the promises annexed to them are
Christ's, and we cannot think that Christ's grace
should be hindered by man's wickedness, or that
because His ministers are not faithful to Christ,
therefore Christ will not be faithful in performing
His promises to His people, which promises were
made not dependent on the administration of the
sacraments by *faithful* persons, but on the ordinances when duly administered. He said a
great deal more, making all this very clear, but I
will go on to the instances he gave us from the
Scriptures. The first was, I think, that of Aaron,
who was made High-Priest immediately after he
had worshipped the Golden Calf ; and, shortly
after his consecration, he and Miriam rebelled

against Moses : yet, when the people murmured
against Moses and ·himself, about the matter of
Korah, and the Lord sent a plague among them
as a punishment, his intercession for them was
accepted.   This certainly is a very remarkable
instance ; for Aaron had committed the same
crime for which the plague was sent among the
people on this occasion : so it could not have been
from his being a *holy man*, but a *true priest*, that
his prayer was heard.   Then, Balaam, as you
know, was a very wicked man, but nevertheless
he was a true prophet.   All his prophecies, in-
cluding that wonderful one respecting our blessed
Saviour, were fulfilled ; which certainly shows us
that the infirmity of the prophet did not destroy
the benefit of God's ordinances.'

' Well but, James, these are Old Testament
examples, I don't know that they have much
reference to us : the Jews, you know, were under
a different dispensation altogether.'

' And you fancy, then, that they were more
highly favoured than we are ? '

' No, no, quite the reverse, I assure you.'

' But, surely, if the wickedness of their priests
did *not* affect the administering of their sacraments, and the efficacy of their prayers, and you
imagine that such is not the case with our priests,
their position would be preferable to ours, for in
all ages, even in the visible church, ' The evil is
ever mingled with the good :' but I will go on to
the New Testament, if that has more weight with
you ; though I would say in passing, that the

more you study the Jewish priesthood, and all
the ordinances connected with it, the more fitted
will you be to understand the Christian priesthood and its sacraments; the latter is, indeed,
only the completion of the former. But now to
the sermon once more. The first instance from
the New Testament, was that of our Saviour
saying to the multitude and His disciples :—"The
Scribes and Pharisees sit in Moses' seat; all
therefore whatsoever they bid you observe, that
observe and do, but do not you after their works;
for they say, and do not." Was not this saying,
—" They are your *lawful* instructors; receive
them as such, but beware of taking them for
your examples?" Now, to make your argument
correct—that we are right in leaving the Church,
if a bad minister is officiating in it—our Saviour
should have said, "The Scribes and Pharisees,
though they sit in Moses' seat, lead such bad
lives, that it would be wrong in you to listen to
their instructions: go and find other teachers,
who will set you a better example:" but, as this
was not His meaning, I think you must allow
that, if they who our Saviour *knew* would not
only reject *His* teaching, but would shortly cause
Him to be crucified, and who could themselves
scourge and mock Him, were yet to be attended
to by the Jews, on account of their *office*, we
surely can have *no* plea for forsaking the Church
on account of the wickedness of any particular
minister. Then, if you want an instance in the
immediate circle of our Saviour's followers, look

at Judas. Our Lord knew that he was to betray Him, and yet to him, as well as to the other Apostles, did He give the commission :—" Go and preach, saying, The kingdom of heaven is at hand. Heal the sick, cleanse the lepers, raise the dead, cast out devils ; " and to him also did He address these words :—" *Whosoever shall not receive you nor hear your words*, when ye depart out of the house, or city, shake off the dust of your feet. Verily I say unto you, It shall be more tolerable for the land of Sodom and Gomorrah than for that city." Can anything be stronger than this, in support of the Twenty-sixth Article of our Church ? Come, Simpson, what do you say, have I satisfied you on this point ? '

' Yes, yes, indeed you have ; I only wish I knew half as much as you do on all these points.'

' Well, if you had been at church last Sunday, you would have heard all this, and a great deal more : I wish I could recollect all Mr. T. said ; but I thought he put the matter very clearly, when he was summing up all he had said.

' " Suppose now," he said, " that a person fell sick, and sent for a physician. The physician, after examining him, says to the patient, ' I see exactly what your complaint is, I will send you some medicines by my servant, and if you will persevere in using them, for a certain time, you will be quite well.' The physician goes away, and sends the medicine by his servant, who happens to be a very wicked man. Would the sick

man be wise to refuse to take the medicine,
because the physician's servant was a bad man?
Is it likely the medicine would change its nature,
and become poison, because it had been carried
a few miles by a wicked person? If the patient
took it, he would certainly recover, but, if not,
he would as certainly die."

'Can you guess, Simpson, what he was proving by this?'

'I think I can, for I know that our Saviour
is sometimes called, "The great Physician of our
souls."'

'Just so; and he went on to say, that He
sends to us His servants, the priests of the
Church, to administer to us the blessed sacraments of His body and blood; that heavenly
medicine which is to heal our souls. He then
asked if we would refuse to receive this medicine,
because the priest of our parish was wicked? If
so, must we not perish?'

'Well, now,' said Simpson, 'that is not amiss,
after all. I did not think that any one of your
ministers could have said anything so good as
that; but is that all?'

'No, no, there is something very particular
yet. He then said, that, in the case of the sick
man, the only thing he had to do was, to see
whether this man who brought the medicine was
really the physician's servant. If he was sure of
that, it was clearly his interest to take the medicine; that is, if he had any confidence in the
skill of the physician; and so he said it was

with us.   If we have faith in Christ for the heal-
ing of our souls ; if we believe the remedies He
has prescribed are sufficient for our recovery ;
then, the only question we have to ask ourselves,
connected with the minister, is this, Am I sure
that the man is a *true* priest who is going
to administer the sacrament to me ?   Has he
been sent by Christ ?   If he has, it is not my
business to inquire whether he is a good or a
bad man : '*to his own Master* he standeth or
falleth." '

   'Of course,' said Simpson, 'he would make
out pretty clearly that he was himself a true
minister (you must excuse my using the word
priest, James, for it has something popish in my
ears).'

   'No, he did not, but *I* can do so, for you
know, Simpson, the ministers of the Church have
all received their authority from the apostles.'

   'How do you make that out ?'

   'I mean that they receive their authority from
the bishops, who can trace their succession to the
apostles :   just as the Jewish priesthood could
trace theirs to Aaron.'

   'And you think that is of consequence, do
you ?'

   'Undoubtedly I do, for out of that line, I
know the ministers must either have been appointed by others, in a manner different from the
custom of the primitive church, or have appointed
themselves, so that, in either case, they can have
no right to the title of *priests ;* I do not wonder

that you do not like the word, Simpson, because none of the dissenters can have the slightest claim to it, excepting the Roman Catholics.'

'But they are not *dissenters*, James.'

'I will prove to you that they *are*, by and by, but I must first finish our good rector's sermon. He remarked that it was a blessed thing for us, that Christ had not made the due celebration of the sacraments to depend upon the holiness of the priests, for then we should never have known whether we had received a sacrament or not. For how can we dive into men's hearts, and see whether they are holy or not? or if He had *always* chosen holy men to be His priests, might we not have been tempted to forget God, and think too much of His servants? perhaps, even to have fallen down and worshipped them, as St. John did the angel; but now, by choosing men of like passions with ourselves to be His priests, the Almighty, who is a jealous God, has effectually prevented this mischief. The infirmity of the men will prevent us thinking too much of them, and the holiness of the *office* ought to make us faithful receivers of the sacraments, which they administer, not in their own name, but in Christ's.'

'Well, really, I do think I will go and hear your rector next Sunday, for there must be a vast deal in his sermons, if all this was in one.'

'Yes it was, indeed, and a great deal more, but pray, Simpson, don't come to hear *him*. Stay away, till you can come *to worship God* in the

words of our beautiful Liturgy, but *don't* come
to hear Mr. T.'

'Well, I see I can't please you, James; I
thought you would have jumped over the moon
at having lured me into the Church once more.'

'Not I, Simpson, indeed, because if it is for
the sermon only you come, you will be off again
to the first new-comer at the meeting-houses.   I
shall be glad, indeed, to see you a constant attendant at the church, and not a mere wanderer.
Do you give me no hope of that, Simpson ?   or
have all my arguments been lost upon you ? if
so, I must get the rector, I think, to take you in
hand.'

'Why, yes, I must say you have cured me
of many of my ignorant prejudices, but still you
have not shown me why I may not, without sin,
dissent from you, as you dissented from the
Romish Church.'

'Wrong   again,   my   friend.   The   Roman
Catholics are the schismatics here, just as much
as the Protestant dissenters ; they split off from
us, just at the same time as the Presbyterians
did.   The Church in England reformed herself:
it was not that *she left* the Romish Church, but
that she purified herself from the corruptions that
crept in during many hundred years. All that our
reformers (as they are called) did, was to get rid
of these corruptions, the chief of which was,
making the Pope supreme head of the Church ;
whereas, Christ is the only *head :* in fact, it was
this error that led to all the others, for as they

made him infallible, (that is, one who could not err,) of course, as might have been expected, the popes, one after another, gave their sanction to many things which the tradition of the Catholic church condemned, and which, at the Reformation, were therefore discarded; but the bishops and priests did not *leave* the church in doing this. Supposing a servant of yours had got into a great many bad habits; was given to drunkenness or idleness, or other bad things, and after being convinced that all this was contrary to his duty, was to leave them off, you would not therefore say, that he had *left* your service?'

'By no means.'

'Well, then, this was the case at the Reformation. The clergy continued, as before, ministers of the same Church; but purified from all those errors which pride, or ambition, or other bad passions, had introduced, contrary to the doctrines of the Apostles, and the practice of the Primitive Church; for, as I told you before, it is the desire of our Church to conform as much as possible to the practice of the *early Christians*. The nearer we are to them the nearer we conceive we are to the right way, as we really do think the Apostles and Fathers of the Church were quite as *likely* to be right as Calvin or Wesley.'

'Well, I think you may be right in that.'

'Indeed, I hope so; at least, if *I* am wrong, the Reformers were wrong too; for they always appealed to the Apostles and Fathers of the

Church, in proof of the errors of the Romish Church.'

'Well, I think I understand now how the matter stood with the Church at the Reformation, and I can fancy that a few might keep to the old errors ; and those, you would say, had dissented from the great mass ?'

'Yes, our rector told me the other day, that out of upwards of seven thousand clergy, there were not two hundred who did not agree to the reforms that were then made.'

'That was very few, to be sure : but I have still one more objection for you to answer. Your *prayers*, and your Creeds, and all that—I must say, I cannot quite fancy them.'

'And why not ? What is your objection to the prayers, first of all ?'

'Oh! they are always the same ; no variety.'

'And that to me,' said James, 'is one of their great excellencies. By having a form of prayer, we know not only to *whom* we are going to pray, but *for whom* and *for what*. The wants of all mankind are in all ages the same, and why should they not be expressed in the same words? Besides, I do think there is a great charm in knowing that you are using the very same words which our fathers and grandfathers before have used, and that the hundreds of thousands who belong to our pure branch of the Catholic Church do often, ' at the same hour, the self-same homage pay.' Surely it gives a greater *unity* to our prayers, to be thus joining in the use of the same Liturgy, in praising and praying to the same God : and when you object to our prayers being always the same, remember you bring an accusation also against the prayer of our Lord and Saviour, who has given us a *pattern* for forms of prayer, which shows us that *He* approved of them ; and I would have you take care, Simpson, lest others, who have less religious feelings than yourself, take up your objection of the prayers of the Church being always the same, and make it an excuse for not daily studying the Scriptures, since *they* also are *always the same*.'

'Now really, James, you are the aptest fellow at turning an argument against one's self I ever knew ; but go on, and let us hear how you defend your creeds.'

'That will not require many words, Simpson. They were the work of the early Church, and were intended as barriers against the introduction of heresy : had there been no heresy, there would have been no creeds ; but, when men asserted false doctrine, the Church, with her usual maternal care, provided for her children a 'form of sound words,' which so plainly sets forth her grand doctrines, that none of her members can, without knowing it, be seduced into error. And do you not see, too, that both in the creeds and prayers we have a safeguard which dissenters have not, (a disadvantage, by the way, which has tended more than anything else to promote the growth of Unitarianism amongst them,) against those faithless ministers who, as we have mentioned before, were certain to be amongst the faithful ones. Let a minister be ever so much disposed to preach false doctrine, the prayers and creeds would contradict his sermon ; so that as long as his hearers attended to the prayers, he could not lead them astray. According to the practice of the Church, the minister cannot even select what chapters he will read out of the Bible, but all the lessons, epistles, and gospels, with the prayers, are so arranged, that every doctrine of our religion comes in its proper order. But I will lend you a little tract or two which will help you. Here is one which will show you how truly scriptural our Liturgy is ; I believe there is not a passage in it which cannot be proved from Scripture. My children and I often amuse ourselves on Sunday evening with looking out some of the references ; and I would advise you to do the same. The tract is called ' *Sunday Exercises*, by the Rev. J. Nicholls.' "

' Thank you, James, thank you. I have learnt more from you than from many Sermons ; but tell me, James, you are convinced that the Church is right, and I must confess that you have done something towards making me think the same : do you then think that those who are not members of the Church cannot be saved ? '

' My dear Simpson, that is a point which it is not for you, or for me, or for any person living to decide. God forbid that we should draw a line which He has not marked out for us. He alone knows their hearts, and knows how far their sin of schism is wilful, or the effect of early prejudice, or other causes. We may charitably hope, I think, that, where it is the latter, God will not be extreme to mark what is done amiss ; but at all events, *our* case is clear ; we have the light, and if we still go on in darkness, *our* condemnation is certain. If we, who *know* that our ministers are divinely commissioned, and that the sacraments are duly administered, refuse to hear the former and to receive the latter, surely *we* must expect that dreadful sentence which our Saviour will pronounce on those who never knew him,—" Depart from me, ye wicked, into everlasting punishment." We know how much greater was the sin of him who *knew* his Lord's will, and did it not, than of him who knew it not, and failed to do it. See then, Simpson, that you and I are not amongst the former ; if we *know* these things, happy are we if we do them.'

CHAPTER VII.

AT the beginning of the conversation related in the last chapter, Susan had slipped away from the fireside, where she had been engaged working, but James was so deeply occupied in his conversation with Simpson that he had not missed her until the latter was going. No sooner had

K

he bid him good-night, than he went into the
next room, to see what had become of her, and
there he found her sitting and leaning over the
baby's cradle, listening attentively to its breathing, with a very anxious countenance. He was
just beginning to laugh at her for slipping away
so slyly, when he observed her distressed look.

'Why, Susan dear, what is the matter; why
do you look so unhappy?'

'Oh, I am so thankful you are come,' said
Susan, 'for I have been longing for Simpson to
go, that I might speak to you.'

'But, dear Susan, why did you not call me?
you know I could have come in an instant, but,
to tell you the truth, you slipped away so quietly
that I never saw you go.   When was it that you
left us?'

'Do not you remember hearing baby cough?'
said Susan.

'No, indeed, I do not.'

'It was very soon after I had set myself down
to my work; and when I came in, she seemed to
me to be breathing so quick, and as if her chest
was oppressed, that I did not like to hear her;
and yet, as I thought it might be only my fancy,
I did not like to disturb you, when Simpson and
you were so earnestly engaged in conversation;
but now you are come, do just listen, and see if
you perceive anything different in her breathing.'

James knelt down by the side of the cradle,
and put his ear close to the child's mouth; Susan
saw by his countenance that he confirmed her

fears, and as he took the infant's hand in his, he said, ' I think, Susan dear, I had better go for the doctor ; this little hand burns very much. It may only arise from the teeth she is cutting, but I think you were saying this morning, that baby had a nasty cough, and if so, we had better not delay getting Mr. Thompson to come and see her. If he considers this heat of no consequence, he will, of course, tell you so, and it will ease your mind, and if otherwise, the sooner the child gets the medicine the better.'

Before Susan had time to reply, James had on his hat, and his hand had opened the door, and in ten minutes the doctor was by Susan's side, whilst the baby, who was just eleven months old, lay on her knee. Mr. Thompson had heard from James a good deal of the child's symptoms, and had fancied that it might possibly be an attack of inflammation, and had brought with him a blister and medicine. Poor Susan looked sadly distressed, when, after examining the child, he took out the blister from his pocket, and said it must be applied immediately. Up to this time, Susan had had no serious illness amongst her children, so that the application of the blister alarmed her more than it would have done those who had been more accustomed to illness.

' Perhaps,' said the doctor, ' it would be better to put the baby in a warm bath, before the blister is put on, and that will be likely to make her sleep while it is drawing.'

James instantly fetched some water, put it on the fire, brought a tub, which Susan generally used for washing the children in, and in a short time the baby was in the bath. Mr. Thompson kindly stopped to see how the child was after the bath, and then gave it the medicine he had brought with him. Poor Susan's heart was too full to ask any questions, but as the doctor was going away, James followed him, and asked him in an under-tone what he thought of the baby.

'The life of an infant,' said he, 'is of course always in danger when anything like inflammation attacks the lungs, but I trust the remedies I have ordered will check its progress. I will be here early in the morning, but, if any unfavourable symptoms come on during the night, be sure to let me know.'

When James returned to the room, Susan saw that he looked pale and agitated, and it was with difficulty she asked him what the doctor thought of her dear baby, who was at that moment sleeping on her lap, breathing in that heavy and hurried manner which no mother can hear without unwelcome thoughts arising as to the possible result. James was silent for a few minutes, but upon Susan's tears beginning to run down her cheeks and to fall on the infant, James tried to rally her. 'The doctor says we must be very regular with the medicine, Susan dear, and, above all, he charged me to tell you not to let the blister be on more than four hours;

whether it is risen or not you are to take it off, as much mischief, he says, is often done by keeping it on longer.'

' And what did he say, James ?   Is our babe in danger ? '

' Why, dear, we need no doctor to tell us, that any illness to so young a child is attended with danger.   In infancy a little matter will often put out the spark of life ; but he hopes that the blister and the medicine together will be of great service to our little one.'

Susan thought she had better not go to bed, at all events, till the blister was taken off, and James said he would sit up with her, and make her some tea, as she had not had her usual supper.   Poor Susan scarcely knew how to swallow the tea, and the bread and butter was a still more difficult task to accomplish ; but James entreated her so much to take care of her own strength, that she might be able the better to nurse the baby, which was not yet weaned, that she managed to drink one cup of tea, and to eat a morsel of bread.   The little infant's rest was very much disturbed by its cough, and the hoarseness of its cry, when awoke by it, distressed poor Susan sadly.   She hoped, however, that, when the blister was removed, it would relieve the cough, as well as the oppression at the chest ; and she watched the minutes till the hands of the clock pointed at two, and then she took off the blister, and after cutting it and put-

ting on the ointment, she advised James to go to
bed, promising to call him if she wanted him.
After much persuasion, James consented to lie
down outside the bed with his clothes on, so
that he might be ready at a moment's notice, if
Susan called.　The other children were all sleeping soundly, not aware of the anxiety which their
parents were suffering on their sister's account,
when their father went into their room to look
at them before lying down himself.　On his
return to his own room, he said to his wife,
'Dear Susan, in our anxiety about this dear
baby, we have forgotten our usual prayers; stay,
I will reach down the Prayer-Book; let us not
forget to thank God for the blessings of the past
day on our other children, and pray that, if it be
His will, this present trial may be removed.'
As he turned over the leaves of the Prayer-Book
with a trembling hand, his eyes fell upon the
prayers at the end of the Visitation of the Sick,
and immediately he was on his knees, and
repeated with great earnestness the following
prayer :—

'O, Almighty God, and merciful Father, to whom alone
belong the issues of life and death, look down from Heaven,
we humbly beseech Thee, with the eyes of mercy, upon this
child, now lying upon the bed of Sickness; visit her, O
Lord, with thy salvation; deliver her in thy good appointed
time from her bodily pain, and save her soul, for thy
mercy's sake; that if it shall be thy pleasure to prolong
her days here on earth, she may live to Thee, and be an
instrument of thy glory by serving Thee faithfully, and
doing good in her generation; or else receive her into those

heavenly habitations where the souls of them that sleep in the Lord Jesus enjoy perpetual rest and felicity. Grant this, O Lord, for thy mercies' sake, in the same thy Son, our Lord Jesus Christ, who liveth and reigneth with Thee and the Holy Ghost, ever one God, world without end.— Amen.'

Susan's tears had glided gently down her cheeks during the greater part of this prayer, occasionally dropping on the gown of the sick infant, for whom it had been offered, but as James concluded, they fell more rapidly, and she struggled to prevent a sudden burst of weeping which might have awoke the infant, by burying her face in her handkerchief. As soon as she could command herself sufficiently, she asked James where he had found that beautiful prayer. ' From our " Common Prayer-Book," Susan. I was looking for our usual prayers when this one, so fitted to our present trouble, caught my eye.'

' I feel better since you read it, James. Oh! may God be pleased to hear it.'

At this moment a violent fit of coughing seized the baby and it appeared nearly choked. James only waited until the cough had ceased, and then, without staying for a word from Susan, he was out at the front door to seek for the doctor. Mr. Thompson, who had been expecting the summons, was down-stairs in five minutes, and putting a couple of leeches in his pocket he was immediately on the road to Susan's cottage. When he got there, he found the child in a sort of stupor, which he feared was the forerunner of death,

but he instantly applied the leeches to the throat,
as Susan said the child had great difficulty in
swallowing when awake ; indeed, the uneasiness
with which the poor little thing then appeared
to breathe, served to confirm the doctor's
previous apprehensions.   Whilst the leeches
were on, the child seemed insensible to the pain
of them, and continued sleeping and breathing
heavily.   Susan watched it with breathless
anxiety, and poor James, whenever it appeared
at all less oppressed at its chest, looked anxiously
at the doctor, to see if he thought at all more
favourably of the little invalid.   Mr. Thompson
shook his head, as if to silence any question from
James ; but, when the leeches were off, he proposed trying the effect of the warm bath again.
The dear child's night-gown was just being
slipped off, and James and the doctor were by
its side to assist Susan in placing it into the
bath, when it fetched a heavy sigh, and all
symptoms of life seemed fled.   The doctor still
wished to see if the warm water would effect
any change, but, alas! the spark was gone, and
nothing earthly could light it again.   Poor
Susan could scarcely believe that all was real,
as it passed before her, till she heard the doctor
say, 'Ah! poor thing, its sufferings here are
over ;' and poor James, with suppressed sobs,
added, 'Thank God, they have been short.'
The considerate doctor knew he could do no
more at that time, and feeling that he might be
a restraint on the feelings of the bereaved parents,

took his leave, having first asked James if he could send any one who would be of service to his wife. James thanked him for his kindness, and begged him to ask Susan's aunt, who lived very near to Mr. Thompson, to come as soon as possible. No sooner had he left the cottage than Susan's tears flowed freely, and she was greatly relieved by them; for her previous state of excitement had been so great, as to deny her this soothing vent to her grief.

Susan's kind aunt very soon arrived, and as she saw the little infant corpse on Susan's knees, she kissed it and dropped a tear, though at the same time, with a degree of energy which was her characteristic, (and which we must remember had led her to take charge of Susan's brother, when left an orphan, in addition to her own large family,) she said, 'Fret not, dear Susan, God has taken away what He lent you, and which He now claims again; and should you not return it without murmuring?'

'I will not murmur, aunt, indeed I will not;' and so saying, she stooped down, and kissing its marble forehead, she faintly said, 'God's will be done;' and whilst her aunt put a clean white gown and little night-cap on the child, James tried to engage Susan in conversation; but she could only weep: so he thought it best to leave her to herself till the first burst of grief was over. Indeed it was only the hope of doing good to Susan that kept him from following her example;

for his heart was full, and when he saw his little
infant looking so unearthly, so pure, so white, so
placid, he took her arm in his, saying, 'Come and
see our little one, my Susan;' and when they
reached the spot on which it lay, they both in-
voluntarily knelt down, and though no sound but
that of sobs was heard by Susan's aunt, doubtless
their prayers ascended to Him, who was at all
times their guide, and would now be their
comforter.

₁ By this time it was seven o'clock, and they
heard the voices of the children, who were as yet
ignorant of what had passed.   Susan tried to
speak: 'Aunt, the children will——' but she
could say no more—her aunt understood her. 'I
will go and tell them, Susan dear; but try to
calm yourself before they come into the room.'

When her aunt went into the children's room,
there was a loud shout of surprise and joy, which
was, indeed, suddenly changed into silence and
sorrow.   'Hush, my dears,' she said, 'you must
be very quiet to-day: your mother is very un-
well.'

'Has she got another baby, then, to show
us?' said Tommy, who had gained great com-
mendation when this poor little infant was born,
as having been the first to guess what present his
mother had received.

'No, my dear Tommy, she has not indeed,
and you will never again be able to nurse your
little baby sister.'

'Oh! aunt, why not? I am sure I am getting *very* big now; you know father said I had grown an inch last week, when he measured me.'

'True, Tommy dear; but your little sister is gone now to be with the angels in heaven.'

'What, aunt, what do you say?' said all the children; 'is our sister gone away?'

'Her spirit is gone, my dear children, and though her little earthly form is still here, she can no longer laugh and crow to you, nor will she cry any more.'

'Oh! aunt, pray let me see her,' said Margaret, still scarcely understanding what had happened.

'You shall, my children, all of you, one at a time, for you must make no noise.'

'Can sister Lucy hear us, aunt, now she is in heaven?' asked Little Tommy; 'I think she won't if we whisper.'

The innocent prattle of her little nephew quite affected his aunt, and she said, 'It is your mother, my dear boy, who cannot bear any noise just now, for she is very poorly.'

'Oh! aunt, why is she ill now? I recollect she was ill when little Lucy was born, but I will be just as quiet as I was then: don't you recollect, you used to let me sit by the side of the fire, with my book sometimes, and rock the cradle?'

Mrs. Burnup (for that was the aunt's name) was tempted to give the children some injunction about not talking of the baby to their mother, feeling how much even she was upset by it, but upon consideration, she thought it best only to repeat her caution of being quiet, and let the rest take its chance. Little Tommy being the most anxious to see his sister, and having a little winning manner with him which few could resist, was taken first into the room. He went in very softly, and seemed quite surprised at finding that his mother was not in bed.

'Are you better, dear mother?' said he, 'for aunt told me you were ill.' She could only answer him with a kiss, and his aunt taking his hand, led him to a corner of the room, where the baby was laid, covered over with a white sheet. When his aunt gently removed it, Tommy (quite forgetting the promised whisper) said, 'Why, aunt, you said Lucy was in heaven, and all the time she is only sleeping; but how pretty and white she looks, do let me kiss her.'—He was just reaching over to do so in his aunt's arms, when his hand touched hers, and its icy coldness made him draw back, saying, 'Oh! aunt, how very, very cold! do lay a blanket over her.'

'Hush, my child,' said his aunt, 'you forget your promise. How loud you speak!'

'But, aunt, Lucy is *not* in heaven, and she is so sound asleep, that you see she does not hear me; why did you say she was gone away, and that I should not nurse her any more? do lay something warm over her, for see, aunt, she has only this thin sheet, and her feet are as cold as her hands.'

Poor Susan burst into fresh sobs, as she heard her little boy's questions, and her aunt was going to take him out of the room, but Susan motioned to her to let him remain, as, though it caused involuntary streams of tears, there was a mournful pleasure in hearing his infantine inquiries. At hearing his mother's sobs, he ran up to her, and putting his little arms round her neck, he said to her, 'Oh! mother dear, why do you cry? Did you not tell me not to cry when I had a pain in my head, but to be patient, because God loved us when we bore pain well: for He makes us ill, doesn't He, mother? I hope He will soon make you well.'

Mrs. Burnup saw that his mother could make no reply, so she said to him, 'Come, my dear boy, you must go now, and let your sisters and brother come and see your mother;' after snatching another peep at little Lucy, he went out of the room, saying, 'I will come again and see you, mother dear, very soon, and I will pray to God to make you better, and not to take little Lucy to heaven yet.'

Margaret and Fanny went in by turns to see their mother. They had never seen a corpse before, and the beauty of their little sister seemed to affect them much, for having had so short an illness, she had lost none of the plumpness of infancy, and looked as if she had been carved out of a piece of white marble. As Fanny approached the infant, and saw it looking so like sleep, she said to her aunt, 'I never thought death could be so pretty, aunt. I am sure the angels will love Lucy, she looks so sweetly.'

'Hush, my dear Fanny,' said her aunt, 'do not talk now, your mother cannot bear it yet; when she is better, she will speak to you all; just kiss her now, and go away.'

As Margaret was going out, she stole to her mother, and just whispered in her ear, that this was her birth-day, and that she must not cry so very much on that day.

'True, dear girl,' said her mother, 'I ought not to do so. You were the first child that God gave me, and on the same day, after ten years of almost constant happiness, He has recalled one, and that one, my infant child: no, I must not, will not murmur; but I cannot talk now, Margaret; in a few hours I shall be better, and I will tell you about some things that I want you to do.'

After Tommy, Fanny, and Margaret had been in, Mrs. Burnup brought in little James, who was only three years old; he was constantly pulling his aunt to take him to stroke 'the poor baby,' as he called her, and, even after he had been taken into the kitchen, he kept knocking at the door, every now and then, to be taken to peep at her.

In the middle of the day, I was passing the cottage, not knowing what had happened, (though James was just coming to tell me,) and was surprised at seeing the half-closed shutters. I tapped gently at the door, and little Margaret opened it.

Her reddened eyelids told me that she had been
crying; and her quiet ' Will you walk in, sir ? '
was so unlike her usual blitheness, and her instant
call to her mother to let her know that I was there,
that I guessed this favoured cottage was now the
place of mourning. ' Is your mother not well,
Margaret ? ' said I.

' No, sir, she is very sadly, sir ; ' a tear starting
in her eye, as she added, ' and our little Lucy is
gone.'

' What do you mean, my dear ? ' said I ;
' where is she gone ? '

' To heaven, sir,' she replied, bursting into
tears ; ' but will you step in, if you please, and
see my mother ? '

' No, Margaret, not to-day ; but tell her I have
called, and say that if she wishes to see me, she
has only to send me word.' As I was going out,
Mrs. Burnup came out of the other room, and
asked me to step in and see the infant corpse,—
she said her niece had heard my voice, and did
not like that I should leave the house without
seeing her ; but she added, ' I doubt she is over
sore troubled to speak to you, sir.' I stepped in
for a minute, but only to say, ' God comfort you,
Susan,' and to shed a tear over the little snow-
drop, for so this little infant looked to me ; and I
hastened out of the room, thinking that my visit
would be better delayed for a few days, till
Susan's grief had become more calm, which I was
sure, from my knowledge of her character, it
would shortly do. Just as I had left the cottage,

I met poor James, and with him was the undertaker, going to take measure for the coffin.

'I have just been at your house, sir,' said
James.

'And I at yours, James,' I replied.

'Ah, sir,' said James, 'you would find it
sadly changed since this day week at this time,
or indeed since yesterday at this hour ; little did
we then think that one of our little ones would so
soon be amongst the angels in heaven. I believe
it will break my wife's heart, sir, indeed I do ;
and it hurts me even more than the loss of the
child to see her take on so, sir ; for we are *sure*
that it's happy, and that is a comfort we cannot
always have at a death ; but Susan seems as if
she could think of nothing of this sort, sir.'

'Do not distress yourself about that, James,
and do not talk to her till you see she is disposed
for it.   In these cases it does no good to force the
feelings ; nature must be allowed to have her way
for a time ; and I believe, that, though you and I
are both fathers, we can neither of us quite understand the depth of a mother's love.   We are
both fond of our children, but with all that, I am
not quite clear that we could go through the daily
privation which mothers do for their children.'

'I believe you are right, sir, at least as far as
my wife is concerned ; I am sure her whole study
is, how to manage best for the children.   While
they are infants, especially, she never has them
out of her sight.'

'Then you see, James, she will of course feel

its loss more than you will, for, in the first place, you are but little at home in the day, and at night you would of course see nothing of the baby, so that the elder children are naturally more interesting to you ; but take my word for it, Susan's present state of excitement will not last long, though you must not expect any great change till after the funeral ; but I will venture to predict, that shortly afterwards you will see her, if not cheerful, at least calm, and able to talk upon the mercy shown her in the manner of her child's departure, for surely nothing can be more painful to a mother than to see her child racked with suffering ; and this Susan has been spared.'

'True, sir, that is indeed a blessing, and I hope she will think so by and by.'

The undertaker had gone to the house, whilst James stood talking with me, and as he recollected this he hurried away, saying that he feared Susan would be terribly agitated at seeing the man, so he must make haste. Poor James ! how different was his countenance on that day from its usual cheerful aspect. In his anxiety for his wife, he tried to forget the loss he had sustained, and to think only of hers ; but it was very evident how great an effort it cost him. When he got home, he was glad to find that the undertaker had not gone into the room, and he contrived to go up to Susan, and conceal what he was doing ; and, as her face was hid in her handkerchief, she did not know that any other

L

person was in the room, till she heard him say, 'Aye, it is a pretty little creature;' but she asked no questions, and the man went out, and James followed him. Towards evening Susan became more composed, and asked James if the day was fixed. At first he did not know to what she alluded, but she pointed to the corner where the child was laid; and he said, 'Yes, dear, next Saturday; this is Tuesday, and I thought that would give you time enough.'

'Time enough!' she said, as if she did not quite understand him.

'Yes, dearest, to make any little preparation.'

'Oh! I understand you now; you mean my mourning; my heart mourns, indeed, but yet I scarcely like to think of black being connected with my angel child. There is nothing mournful with her, no, only in my heart, and that no one sees but God: she is perhaps now joining the infant cherubs in their songs of praise, and I, I am weeping.'

'Dear Susan, if you think so, if you believe her to be thus blest, will you, her mother, repine at her happiness? When she has gained so much, will you grieve at your own loss? That is not like the mother of my children. How often, when I have urged you not to do something, which I thought would hurt you, have you checked me by saying, 'It is for the children's good:' and what greater good do you or I desire for them than fitting them for that blessed place, where we trust our sweet baby

now dwells? Is it not for this that we daily
pray? And bitter as is the first parting from
our child, think how much deeper would be our
affliction, had we felt any fear of her future happiness. Do think of this, Susan dear, and of
many other mercies which you may see in this
trial.'

'Yes, James, I will,' said Susan, sobbing
violently: 'I will try; but you do not know,
indeed you do not, a mother's feeling, the wrench-
ing of the heart-strings which the loss of a child
is to her; I know it only by suffering it.'

'I grant it fully, Susan, but I know too that
in such suffering, we are taught to look to Him
who has said, " Call upon me in the day of trouble,
and I will hear thee," and I am sure you will *call*
upon Him.'

'Yes, James, I will indeed. Oh! what must
those suffer who know not what it is in such a
trial to have *One* to fly to who knows *all* our
griefs, and will support us in bearing them. But,
James, "Jesus wept "at the grave of a friend whom
He was going to restore, and may not I weep at
the grave of my child—my own baby, who only
three days ago was in perfect health? I do not
repine, James; I can think of my babe's happiness till my heart breaks forth into thankfulness;
but then comes in weak nature, and I weep as I
miss her from my breast; in short, James, a cord
is broken, which can never be re-united in this
world.'

'Yes, Susan, but, if that one link of the chain

which binds you here is broken, has it not been added to the chain which draws you towards heaven? If we have lost something that has made the world less dear to us, has it not made heaven still more precious to us?'

'Say no more now, James, my thoughts are too wandering and confused to remember all you say.'

James went away, and having made Susan a cup of coffee, he was pleased to see her take it; and after reading a few verses to her from the 14th chapter of Saint John, and the usual prayers, they went to bed.

CHAPTER VIII.

MRS. BURNUP had gone home after the children's bed-time, but came early the next morning, when she was pleased to find Susan more composed, and able to talk about the work which she would require to have done before the funeral. Little Margaret and Fanny were of the greatest use to their poor mother on this occasion, and hemmed the frills for her caps, and did several similar jobs. In the afternoon the undertaker brought the coffin: this was a sad trial to the feelings of all in the house. Poor James, who had before done his utmost to support his wife, now wept outright, as he saw his infant child placed in its narrow bed, from which it never more would move till the last trumpet sounds. As to Susan, it seemed as if her heart would burst, and the children caught the infection, and sobbed bitterly.

Mrs. Burnup was the first to compose the children, and took them out of the room, excepting Tommy, who would cling to his mother, asking her, who would show Lucy the way to heaven, for she was so little that she could not take care of herself, and he was sure *she* could not know the way, because *he* did not who was so much bigger. Then he began to kiss his mother, and tell her not to cry, and asked her if she would cry when *he* went to heaven; for if she would, he would not pray to God to take him there, for he did not like her to cry so. This speech of the child had more effect in rousing Susan than anything James or his aunt had said, and as she pressed him to her bosom, she said, 'You must pray, dear Tommy, that we may *all* go there, and then we shall see dear Lucy again.'

'Oh! mother, how happy we shall be then,' said this artless child, 'but we must be all *very* good to go there, must not we, mother? It is not good to *cry*, is it, mother?'

Susan smiled through her tears at this arch reproof of her child, saying, 'You cry when you are punished, don't you, Tommy?'

'Yes, mother, but you are so *big*, you have no one to punish you.'

Just as Susan was beginning her reply to this remark, Mrs. Burnup called Tommy to tea, and he skipped away, quite unconscious of the change which his infantile questions had made in Susan's thoughts. James then began to talk to her about whom they should ask to follow their little one to the grave. 'I have been thinking,' said he, 'of inviting Simpson, as he was here when our dear babe's illness was commencing, and in his present turn of mind perhaps it may not do him any harm to bring this beautiful service before him. What say you, Susan dear?'

'I can have no objection, James; all I wish is, that we have as few as possible: let all be done quietly. I could not, indeed, bear the bustle and fuss which is so general at such times. No, no, let us ask those only who will mourn and weep with us.'

'Your aunt intends to go, and she has written to your brother to come over. I have been turning it over in my mind, whether to let the dear girls be present, but I think they had better not. There is no use in overstretching their feelings, and at their tender age it might do harm, especially to our quick little Margaret. Fanny would stand it better, perhaps, but I could not take her without her sister, so I think it is better to say nothing about it: so we shall just be four, Susan dear; that will not be too many for you.'

'Four?' said Susan; 'let me see, how is that! I believe I cannot even count right; let's see. There's your mother and aunt, two; and you and Simpson; that's four; and——'

'Well, dear, that is all.'

'No, James, you forget the chief mourner, your own wife. Yes, I must see the last of my little one. I must see her placed in her last resting-place. I went with her the first and only time that she was taken to the church, and shall I not go with her the *last* time? Shall I go to the church to rejoice over my child, and shall I not go to mourn over her?'

'I fear, Susan dear, it will be too much for your feelings, that is all, for you know how deeply affecting the service is.'

'I know it, James, I know it; but, as it has been provided by the Church for the sad occasion, sure I am that it must suit our feelings and our wants at that time. Yes, I must go—oh! my darling child! Never have I been parted from you, and the grave only shall separate us!'

She again burst into tears, and James said no more on the subject to her, but, after consulting with Mrs. Burnup, it was agreed to let her follow the bent of her wishes, and if, when it came to the point, she began to waver, they might then dissuade her more easily, and if not, they determined to say nothing more about it. As little was said to Susan as possible about the funeral, for James saw the tears start whenever it was alluded to; but Mrs. Burnup made every necessary preparation, aided by little Margaret and Fanny. The trying day at length arrived! that

day which would make Susan feel that her child
was gone indeed; for, as long as we have the
earthly form to gaze on, pale and lifeless though
it be, we seem still to possess a portion, if not *all*
of our treasure, and we look at it again and again,
feeling that *still* it is ours, though the spirit is
gone to Him who gave it. But, when once the undertaker does his office, and there can be no more
gazing, and when in solemn tones the Church
does hers, and we hear, ' Dust to dust, and ashes
to ashes,' and see the earth covering over what
was once ours, then it is we feel, that not even
the outward form remains to us. Poor Susan
summoned up all her fortitude on this trying occasion, and, contrary to my expectations, supported herself wonderfully during the time she
was in church; but, when the coffin was placed
in the ground, and the sexton commenced his
office as I had finished mine, her maternal feelings were uncontrollable, and it was with difficulty
that James and Mrs. Burnup got her home. She
told me, however, afterwards, that she would not
on any account have missed the service, deeply
as she was affected by it, and that whenever she
felt the loss of her baby the most, she used to
go to her Prayer-book, and find the greatest
comfort in reading over the Burial Service.

On the Monday after the funeral, I went to
see Susan, and though there were evident marks
of her having been weeping, I was pleased to
find she could command herself sufficiently to
talk to me on her late loss.

I am glad to see you, sir,' said she, 'for I fear I gave you but a bad reception, but you would excuse me, knowing the cause. The loss of a child, sir, baby though it be, plays such havoc with one's senses, that I believe, for a day or two, I hardly knew what I did or said; but, God be thanked, I am better now, though the tears are here still, but I trust I am not sinful in weeping for my child; for, it is not that I would wish to bring her back to earth: no, no, I am not so selfish as that, but my eyes sadly miss her sweet smiles, and then come the tears.'

'Susan,' I said, 'trials would not be such to us, if we could receive them unmoved: all that we have to do, is to pray for entire submission to God's will, to make our Saviour's prayer our own, "Not my will, but thine be done," and then we need not fear that God will be angry at the infirmity of· the flesh, which accompanies the prayer. He who *knows* our sufferings will help us, Susan, to bear them. He will not forsake us unless we forsake Him; but there is one caution, which, perhaps, may not be quite needless under your present distress. You have lost *one* child, do not in consequence make idols of the rest. Do not forget that they belong to Him who has already called one to Himself, and that they, sooner or later, will also be claimed by Him.'

'Oh! sir,' said Susan, 'I hope I shall not forget this again. I fear I have looked upon them too much as *my own*, and, whilst I have done my best to train them up as true members

of Christ and children of God, I have not felt
that they might at any hour be claimed by their
rightful owner; but now I trust I shall not forget
it, and I am sure my heart will feel doubly
thankful each night and morning that I am
allowed to retain these little ones. I believe,
sir, we do not know the real value of blessings
till we lose a portion of them.'

'I suspect you are right, Susan, in thinking
so, and you may be sure that if we had not these
trials to turn our hearts *wholly* to our Maker
(for I fear we never do it so fully as in trouble),
that we should be very likely in the midst of
blessings to forget who was the Giver of them.'

'Why, sir, it's too true, indeed; but, after
this affliction, we shall be doubly sinful if we do
not thank God for preserving our other children,
when we have felt what it is to lose one! But,
sir, we are too apt to forget these things when
the time of affliction is past, and we do not feel
our utter helplessness without God. I am sure,
sir, I can say with truth, that, as I have stood by
the side of my babe's lifeless form, and of others
before, I have felt that we must indeed be foolish
to think anything precious in this world compared to the next, when we must so soon lose
them : and I have fancied that nothing would
again interest me here; but, sir, it is quite
otherwise after a time, for the same cares and
anxieties, and the same hopes and fears about
worldly things, arise, and I almost forget that I
have stood by the bed of death.'

'Well, Susan,' said I, 'under certain regulations this feeling is planted in us by One who is wiser than we, for His own good purposes. As long as we are in the world, it is our duty to be interested in it, and it is a merciful dispensation, that the distress which the loss of friends causes, does *not* last in its first bitterness, for if it did, how could we perform our duty to our family, our neighbour, or our Maker? But what we ought to do is, to keep in mind our Saviour's rule on the subject, and then we cannot get very far wrong. "Seek ye *first* the kingdom of God and his righteousness." This is the point we should always aim at; but the misfortune is, that we are inclined to seek *every* other thing *before* this, and therefore it is no wonder if our prayers are unheard by God; for if we only give Him the few moments which we cannot conveniently fill up with worldly care, or worldly pleasure, do you think He will accept that? No, Susan, no; if we take the world for our master, we know what will be the consequence, for we have been plainly told that we cannot serve God and Mammon, and that God is a "*jealous* God."'

'Ah, sir,' said Susan, 'here lies the difficulty after all; it is very easy to *talk* and to feel sure that God has said all this, but the difficulty is to keep it so continually before us, as to make it always the *motive* in all we do. We all say that we wish to please God, but I am afraid we too often prove by our actions, if not by our words, that we wish to please the world also.'

'Yes, Susan, it is too often the case, and we should be constantly on our guard against it ; but I have paid you a longer visit than I intended, so good bye. I see your little girls and Tommy running home from school, and they will be wanting their dinners, I dare say.'

CHAPTER IX.

SIMPSON came in a few evenings after this, and had a little conversation with James, but as Susan was still suffering from the effects of her late sorrow, and was greatly affected at seeing Simpson, (remembering the last evening on which he had come for discussion,) James only talked to him that night about the Burial Service. James observed how very appropriate the sentences were which the clergyman read, as he met the corpse at the church-yard gate, and preceded it into the church. First, the assurance of the resurrection, and then the wholesome remembrance, that as we brought nothing into the world, so we can take nothing out ; and, that as it was the Lord who '*gave*,' so it was the Lord who ' taketh away : ' and who will dare to repine at any loss when he hears these words ?

'And yet,' said Simpson, 'I have observed many an eye weep at a funeral, when these words are read, which was dry before.'

'Very likely,' said James, 'but tears are often the bursting forth of gratitude, mingled though it may be with sorrow; for, the greater the loss of our friends to ourselves, the more likely are we to derive comfort from these sentences, so full of instruction to us, and of hope for them.'

'Well, I dare say it is so, and I must say the Psalms are both of them very beautiful, and very impressive at such a time: by the by, James, how is it that people never seem to know what to do at the reading of them, whether to sit, or to stand? I am sure I sometimes feel quite awkward; I should say that we ought to stand: is it not so?'

'Indeed, I think there can be no doubt of the propriety of doing so, and, if it was not that you have such strange customs at many of your meeting-houses, I fancy there never would be any hesitation; but, when you never think of kneeling when you pray, and often sit when you sing, it is not surprising that you are at a loss.'

'But I suppose, James, you think it right to sit when the lesson is read.'

'Oh! undoubtedly; we are then receiving instructions out of the Bible from the priest, and it is therefore quite right that we should sit and receive it, though I believe the time was, when people did not think it too great an exertion to stand during the *whole* service; which, by the by, reminds me of a circumstance that occurred to me when I was a young man, and was servant in Mr. William's family in London. The rector of our parish was what is called a *popular* preacher, that is, many people came from other parishes to hear him, and, consequently, there was great difficulty in getting seats, but as my master lived in the parish, there was a pew for us, as his servants. It happened that one morning, from some cause, which I have forgotten, I did not get into the church till the minister had commenced his sermon. The text was just given out—the aisles were crowded to excess—all eyes were fixed on the clergyman: I saw that my seat was unoccupied, and I began to push my way through the dense mass of people between me and the pew. I had got about half way, when I found myself close to an elderly gentleman, whose grey hairs and venerable appearance seemed to give him a right to reprove a youth like myself, who was entering thus thoughtlessly the house of God. Seeing that he did not move when I came close to him, I whispered to him that I wanted to get to my seat: with a look which I shall never forget, and a tone that now sounds in my ear, he said, motioning with his hand to the pulpit, "Don't you see the clergyman is standing?" I cannot describe to you, Simpson, the instantaneous effect which these words had on me; it was more like magic than anything else; and I believe I shall feel its good effects until my dying day. As to moving, I could not: in the self-same spot I stood till the sermon was ended, stirring neither hand nor foot; and what was the *most* extraordinary thing, I felt no fatigue, for, like my friendly reprover, my attention became riveted on the preacher, and it convinced me that if we were only really engaged in serving God, and gave our *whole* souls to that, we should not take so much thought as we do about making our *bodies* comfortable at the same time.'

'Well,' said Simpson, ' that is as good a story of the kind as I ever heard, and I don't think I shall forget it in a hurry; but there. is one thing, or, as I may say, two, in your " Burial Service," which we were talking of just now, that I cannot quite reconcile to myself. Here, just hand me your Prayer-Book : this is the first place which I mean—it is in the prayer beginning " Forasmuch as it hath pleased Almighty God, &c.;" you go on to say, " We therefore commit his body to the ground, earth to earth, ashes to ashes, dust to dust, *in sure and certain hope of the resurrection* to eternal life, through Jesus Christ our Lord." '

'Well,' said James, 'what is there in that expression that you object to?'

'Why, it is not the expression itself that I object to, but that it is often said over those who we can hardly believe will rise to life eternal.'

' But the prayer, Simpson, expresses no opinion as to the salvation of the person then interred, but only our " *hope* of *the* resurrection to eternal life." '

'Oh! I see now that it is not *his* or *her* resurrection; to be sure that does make a difference which I never thought of; but in the last prayer, however, you do express a *hope* of *the* person's salvation.'

'Well, Simpson, do we not in many cases hope almost against belief? we may hope even though fear be mingled with it. Charity, you know, "hopeth all things," and surely on this subject we ought to be cautious of forming harsh judgments, remembering that, when the prophet Elisha thought that *he* alone worshipped God, it turned out that there were seven thousand in Israel who had not bowed the knee to Baal: and may it not be so with many who, we fancy, have not died the death of the righteous? We certainly may know that their actions have not been what they should have been, but at the same time we do *not* know what is resisted. He alone who knew of the seven thousand in Israel, knows who are His now, and I cannot think that it becomes us to form any judgment on the subject. Our part is, to see that we neglect nothing to make our own death, and that of those dear to us, an entrance to eternal life through the merits of our merciful Redeemer, who could pray that His *murderers* might be forgiven, and therefore has surely taught us to hope (in some cases) even against hope.'

'Well, James, you have studied all these things much more than I have; what then do you think of that passage in which you give

God hearty thanks, for that it hath pleased Him
" to deliver this our brother out of the miseries
of this sinful world ? " '

'What do I think of it ?   Why, I think of it,
as I do of every portion of our service, that it is
fitted to our feelings and wants at the time in a
wonderful manner.   What do you think com-
forted me most when I lost my child ?   Why,
the certainty of its present and future happiness,
and that it was saved many miseries in this sinful world ; and so it is, Simpson, in every trial
that befalls us, painful as it may be to flesh and
blood ; there is always a *something* for which we
have to be thankful.   " In all things let us give
thanks," is my motto; for it keeps one's mind in
such a happy state : and you see, in the prayer
before us, the Church fixes on the *very* thing to
be thankful for, which is equally applicable to
all, under all circumstances, to high and low,
rich and poor, old and young ; for miseries there
are for all of us, whilst we are in a sinful world.
This is what my master used to call the *Catholic*
spirit of the Church in all her services. Catholic,
you know, means " universal," or suited to *all ;*
and so are her services, as you will find out, if
you will only study them.'

'Well, now you've stumbled on the very
word I have so often wanted to ask you about ;
why, I thought the Papists were the Catholics.'

'No, no, they are called *Roman* Catholics,
though it is an odd jumble of a name ; but you
know we express our belief in " the Holy Catho-

M

lic Church" every time we say the Creed; and if we are members of that, as I trust I am, we are certainly Catholics.'

'But,' said Simpson, 'you don't worship images, and pray to saints, and all that sort of stuff, do you, like those other Catholics?'

'No,' said James, somewhat impatiently, 'you don't understand me, or perhaps you do not see the difference between *Roman* Catholics and Catholics. The Romanists—for I think that is a better term—consider the Pope as the *universal* bishop; that is, that all other bishops, priests, and deacons in the world are under him, and also that he is Christ's representative on earth. Now *we* assert that Christ's Church is *universal* or Catholic, and that He is the universal bishop over it; but that every true branch of the Church is governed by bishops, priests, and deacons, and all the members of the universal or Catholic Church are consequently Catholics.'

'Ah! I see now the meaning of the word; I never did understand it before; but I must go now, perhaps some other day I may talk to you again on the subject.'

CHAPTER X.

I HOPE my readers will excuse the long digressions I have often made in this narrative, as I am anxious they should understand, as fully as possible, all the opinions of James and Susan (for what were his were hers also), as I do not think I ever met, in high or low, so much thought, and such sound judgment: he seemed as if you could not put him off his guard. Nothing merely plausible had any weight with him; it must be on sound principles, or he would have nothing to do with it; and he had such a quiet way of refusing to join in anything of which he did not approve, that no one could be offended with him.

The Box Clubs he would never have anything to do with, though · he always warmly advocated the Savings' Bank, and the Friendly Institution, which have all the benefit of Box Clubs, without any of the risk. I must not omit his opinion on Temperance and Teetotal Societies, though perhaps some of my readers may not be pleased that he did not join either the one, or the other. When he was asked to sign the book one day by a friend, he seemed very thoughtful for a moment, and then looking him earnestly in the face, he said,—

'My good fellow, did you ever see me intoxicated, or in any way the worse for liquor?'

'Never,' replied his friend, 'but would it not be as well to put yourself out of the way of temptation?'

'Oh! certainly, but I don't see how signing the book will put me out of the way of temptation.'

'Don't you? Why, if you make a vow never to taste spirituous liquors, how can you possibly become intoxicated?'

'True, my friend, but supposing I have already something (which is much more binding than any pledge to man) that tells me, that "Drunkards God will judge," that *no* drunkard will inherit the kingdom of God, (and all this, and much more to the same purpose the Bible tells me,) I cannot see how I can have any higher motive for abstaining from intoxication: if the thought that God sees me at all times is not a check on my intemperance, I cannot think that my signing your book would be likely to be so: besides, my friend, don't you see that I should be *throwing* myself into temptation? I can *now* take a glass of beer very innocently (having no vow upon me); *then* I could not do so without a *great sin;* and what should I gain? I believe nothing, unless it be an additional quantity of self-conceit.'

'Well, but James,' said his well-meaning friend, 'see the good these societies have done. Look at the reformations they have made in confirmed drunkards.'

'I am truly glad of it, in one sense, and I grieve at it in another. I rejoice that any bad habit is corrected in a fellow-creature, but I mourn that the fear and love of God, is not the principle which has led to the reformation. I am an old-fashioned fellow, you know, and anything new-fangled is out of my way; so don't ask me to join in anything which is to be carried on by vows and penances, or you will make me think the Pope has sent you amongst us. My baptismal vows are enough for me, and I desire to make no others. Our Saviour certainly drank wine (for he was jeeringly called a wine-bibber), and even performed his *first* miracle to make some; so *He* did not think that there was any harm in it : and I do not imagine that He would have instituted the Lord's Supper with wine, if He considered it *sinful* to drink it at other times. And indeed, my dear friend, I do think, when you consider the dangerous lengths to which Teetotallers have gone, that they have even *refused* to receive the Lord's Supper, *because* they dared not touch wine, it ought to make them pause in their career. There is something awful in the thought, that a mere human contrivance should be deemed of greater importance than a positive command of our Saviour, the regular performance of which, I suspect, would go further than anything else, to banish drunkenness and all other sins of so deadly a kind from our nation.'

'But has it done so?' said his friend, rather warmly.

'No,' said James; 'for a very good reason,

because Christ's command is *not* obeyed ; because numbers, as you know, leave the church when the sacrament is administered. All I say is this— let us use Christ's ordinances *first*, and when they fail in making us " sober," it will be time enough to frame some of our own.'

'By the by,' said James, in that peculiarly dry manner which he sometimes assumed, ' it never struck me till this moment that the Teetotallers refusing the sacrament because of the wine, does look *very* popish indeed ; for you know the Papists deny the cup to the common people.'

James told me that his friend, on hearing this, looked perfectly horrified ; and, after observing that he certainly had the strangest way of putting things, wished him a hasty good night, and took care never to advocate Teetotalism again in his presence.

CHAPTER XI.

IT is now high time that I should return to Susan, for in my fondness for writing of James I have been neglecting her—perhaps it is, that, as she had a succession of troubles after her baby's death, my pen does not glide so freely as when I had to tell of my light-hearted and blithe-faced Susan ; and yet it was as the suffering Christian, that her character shone in its brightest lustre.   It was at time, too, that I was the most interested in her, as much of her former goodness had been related to me by others; but of this I was an eyewitness, and in some instances, I hope, assisted in comforting her. I think it was not more than six weeks after the death of the infant, that I was called to the sick-bed of Susan herself, who was then suffering from typhus fever. It was a very serious attack, and, when I was first called in to see her, I had no expectation that she would recover, but there was a sweet calmness about her, which showed that she was prepared to die though not unconcerned about living. When I went in, the neatness of the room struck me, and, as little Margaret was putting the last cup in its place when I entered, I saw that she had been brought up in all the tidy ways of her mother; for the room was swept and dusted, and the bed was only exceeded in whiteness by the poor sufferer herself, and she was of that ghostly paleness which is generally the attendant of that fearful disease. Poor Susan! I could not help observing how differently she looked now from what she did the first time I saw her—then she was all vigour and activity—now she was lying powerless and weak. The height of the fever had passed away, during which time she had been quite delirious, and, on her coming to herself, her first request was, that I might be sent for. On my inquiring if Margaret was sole nurse, I found that good Mrs. Burnup had been with Susan during the first part of her illness, but had been called to Liverpool, where one of her sons,

a sailor, had arrived in ill-health, and was not
expected to live.   Little Margaret had, therefore,
begged to take her place, and, to judge from
appearances, seemed likely to supply it well.
On my asking Susan how she felt, she said that
she had no pain now, and she was very thankful
for that; ' but, sir,' she said, 'I am *very*, very weak,
I doubt whether I shall ever regain my strength ;
pray for me that I may have patience to bear my
lot, whatever it may be.   If I live, I hope it will
be a benefit to my little ones, and if I die, I
know Who will provide for them.'   Her voice
was so weak, as she said this, that I could
scarcely understand her, but I did as she desired ;
and, when I had finished, as I bade her good bye
(for I feared to prolong my visit in her weak
state) she said with a sweet smile, ' Thank you,
thank you, I am very happy—yes, if I live, I
hope I shall live unto the Lord, and if I die I
hope I shall die unto Him, so that whatever
happens, I trust I shall be His! '   I begged her
to say no more, but promised to repeat my visit
in a day or two, when I hoped she would be
better able to talk ; for I saw she had exhausted
herself.   How often, when I leave such a scene
of sickness and happiness united, have I wished
that many of my thoughtless flock could behold
it with me, and then contrast it with the state of
a person who has never thought of a Saviour, or
Judge, in the time of health.   How many of
them might be led by it to strive after those
things, which, unlike all earthly things, become

the most valuable when *every* thing else becomes
worthless, and which will endure as long as
eternity itself!

For many days I continued to visit Susan,
without perceiving any material change take
place, either for the better or the worse. I confess, I often left the room fearing each visit might
be the last : nature seemed to make no effort to
rally, and I could not but dread the long continuance of such excessive weakness. During
the whole time, I never heard a murmur escape
her lips; and, when she could say anything beyond joining in the prayers, it was to express
her thankfulness at the good management of
little Margaret and Fanny, and at their having
escaped the fever. 'If I go, sir,' she one day
said to me, 'I believe Meggy will be almost as
much of a mother to the younger ones as myself
—she is so thoughtful, sir!' This, however,
was not to be : and after the daily watchings
and anxieties which poor James had suffered, he
had the happiness to see her begin once more to
have a relish for her food ; and, when he heard
her saying that she could eat a bit of chicken
for dinner, he was so delighted that he came
running up to the parsonage to see if we had
one, as there was not one ready killed in the
village, and he wanted it directly. Most luckily
we had a couple hanging up in the larder, and,
in spite of the black looks of the cook, who was
in the midst of preparing a dinner, of which
the chickens were to form part, my wife had

the pleasure of putting them into James's hand; and in such a hurry was he to run off with them, that he did not stay to hear half of the injunctions my wife was giving him, not to let her eat too heartily at first, for fear of doing her harm, after fasting for so long a time.   From this hour Susan 'turned the corner,' as the nurses say, and her husband and herself were so full of thankfulness at her returning health, that they could think of nothing else.   I can now see poor James, with happy face, leading his wife (still pale from her late illness) to her usual seat at church.   I could not help fancying that they joined with even more than their ordinary devotion; and at the thanksgiving, when I returned thanks publicly for 'the late mercies vouchsafed to her,' I saw large tears stream down the cheeks of both of them.   For a few days health seemed restored to this happy family, but, alas! it was only for a few days; the disease to which poor Susan had been so long a prey had not taken its departure from their fire-side; it had only stayed its progress for a time, and then it appeared in four-fold strength, for one after another were all the children seized, and, though a week intervened between the commencement of the illness in each child, they were all, for a short time, occupying their beds together.   Like the first snowdrops, which so often are seen languidly drooping their heads on the snow which surrounds them, so did these four little creatures lie in their white beds, almost as in-

animate and sickly-looking as those pale flowers.
When I saw Susan in the midst of them, I asked
her if she did not find that they required more
attention than she could pay them herself.

'Oh! no, sir,' she said, 'I can do very well
—besides, all the neighbours are frightened of
us, now that they see the fever is spreading, and
I should be sorry to be the means of giving it to
any of them.' 'But you must take care,
Susan,' said I, 'that you do not lay yourself up
again by your nursing and sitting up at night,
for that would be worse than all.' 'It would,
indeed sir,' she said, 'but James and I take it
in turn to sit up at night, for his master is so
good as to let him come home earlier at night,
and go later in the morning, in order to give
him time for a little more rest; and, indeed, sir,
it comes harder on him than it does on me, for
he has hardly recovered the effects of his sitting
up when I was ill, and then you know, sir, he
has much more work during the day than I
have; but he keeps up his spirits wonderfully,
sir, or rather, I should say, the Lord supports
him, for he is so thankful at my recovery, that
he says he ought never to be distrustful or de-
sponding any more, when he remembers what
trouble God has helped him through.' 'Well,
Susan, it is a happy thing for you, that you have
a husband who can think so rightly. If we all
of us reflected on God's *former* goodness to us,
we should not be so anxious and concerned about
the *future,* as we often are: but we are too apt

to dwell on our troubles, without remembering the mercies which attended them ; whereas, if we did but look at things properly, we should find that our God is, indeed, a God of mercy.' ' Yes, sir, indeed I have cause to say so, even at this moment. Often, as I sit in this room, and look at these four dear children lying so helpless, I ask myself what I should have felt, had *my* illness happened now instead of before my children's : it might have occurred so, or they might have had *no* mother to wait on them, had not our merciful Father ordered it otherwise.' ' True, Susan, they might, indeed ; and so you see that even with a raging fever in your house, you have great cause for thankfulness.' ' I have indeed, sir, and I trust I shall never forget it.' For several days after this visit, I was not able to go and see Susan ;.and, when I did go, I found she had been suffering great anxiety about her two eldest children : poor Margaret, in particular, had been at the very brink of death ; but the whole party seemed to be improving, excepting poor Susan, who bore evident marks of her watching and anxiety. James came in whilst I was there, looking sadly pale and worn out, and, at the time, I really feared that he was marked out as the next victim of this sad disease, but fortunately it proved otherwise. ' Well, James,' I said, ' you have had your hands full lately.' ' Yes, sir, indeed we have ; I am sadly afraid Susan will be knocking herself up again, though, God be thanked, I believe we have passed the

worst of the illnesses, and that gives us strength
to go on. My master has been very kind, and
given me a great deal of time at home to help
her, and now, sir, he has forbidden me to go to
my work for a week, so that I may recover a
little of my sleep, and help Susan at the same
time.' 'That is very kind of him, indeed,
James, and I hope you and Susan will really
devote the week to nursing yourselves, as well
as your children.'

'Yes, sir, we must do so,' said James, ' for
I have been hardly fit for work at all during the
last month, and, if I were to get laid up, that
would be worse than all, after the waiting on
the children that Susan has already had.'

From this time the children got gradually
better, and Susan and James recovered their
looks as the children did theirs.

CHAPTER XII.

AFTER spending three months at Liverpool, Mrs.
Burnup returned home, having attended the
death-bed of her son, and followed him to the
grave. She was sadly shattered by all the fatigue
she had undergone, and the anxiety she had suffered, and was so altered in her appearance that
Susan was quite distressed. She soon perceived,
also, that much of her aunt's former activity was

gone, and that she was not able to attend to her household concerns as she had formerly done, and therefore begged her at once to come, and make her house her home; but this Mrs. Burnup could not be prevailed on to do.

'No, my dear Susan, not as long as I can do for myself will I be a burden to you, with your little family : the time *may* come, God knows, when the poor-house, or yours, will have to be my asylum; but if so, I trust it will not be for long.'

'My dear aunt,' said Susan, 'how can you talk in this way? Is it possible for you to be a *burden* to me? you who have done so much for me and my brother? If you were to live a dozen years with me I should only pay you a small portion of the debt we owe you: and as to my little family—why they will *help* me to wait on you. If you will but come, Margaret will be proud to be your "little maid," and read to you, and talk to you, or work for you, and do whatever you bid her.'

'My dear Susan,' said good Mrs. Burnup, 'say no more; I am an old woman, and you know obstinacy is the privilege of old people; come to you I will not, as long as I can go about my own little cottage.'

'Then, aunt, Margaret shall come and sweep your room every morning. Come, don't say *no* to this, for I must be positive now.'

Little Margaret was delighted at hearing of her new employment, for she was very fond of her aunt. She had for some time had the job of sweeping and dusting at home, but now it was to descend to little Fanny, who was equally pleased in her turn to be made useful to her mother. Margaret was at this time between ten and eleven, and Fanny between nine and ten. Not many weeks after this, when Margaret was performing her daily sweeping at her aunt's, having first made the brass candlesticks so bright that her aunt was quite proud of them, she was alarmed, on asking a question two or three times over, as her back was turned to her aunt, to find that she did not answer her; and, on going to her chair, she perceived that she was quite senseless and unable to move. Margaret called to a little girl, who was passing, to stay with her aunt for a few minutes, whilst she ran as fast as her legs could carry her, to her mother; and, when she got to the house, she was so much out of breath, and so much agitated, that it was with difficulty her mother could understand what had happened; but she quickly slipped on her bonnet, and set off for Mrs. Burnup's house, calling at the good doctor's as she went. As soon as he saw her leaning back on her chair, unconscious of all that was going on, and with her face drawn on one side, he told Susan that it was a paralytic seizure, and that she must immediately put her to bed. Susan thought it would be better if she could be removed to her house, as there she would be able to attend to her constantly. Mr. Thompson hesitated at first, thinking it would be incurring a

risk to move her in her present state; but, upon
Susan's saying that she could get a cart and place
a mattress in it, he consented, and was so kind
as to wait and assist in conveying her to Susan's
cottage, where she was soon placed in a comfortable bed; for Susan gave up her own to
her. But poor Mrs. Burnup was quite unconscious of all the kind attention of her friend.
For a whole week there seemed no symptom of
returning consciousness, or the power of speech;
but at the end of that time she made an attempt
at speaking, but it was so indistinct that Susan
could not make it out, and this distressed her
very much. She was anxious, too, that her aunt
should have the comfort of knowing that she was
not left to the care of strangers. It was therefore with no little delight she went to the bed-
side, from the fire-place, where she was seated
with her work, on hearing Mrs. Burnup softly
mutter, 'Susan, Susan, when will you come?'
With great caution she placed herself by her
aunt, not daring to speak, lest it might prove too
much for her, and not knowing whether she
would recognize her. At first the poor invalid
gazed fixedly on the face of Susan; gradually
her features acquired more expression, and at
last she took hold of her hand, saying in a broken
manner, 'I thought—you would—come—Susan
—when you—knew I was so ill—yes—I am
very—bad.' Susan knew it would not be right
to enter into any explanation at that time of
what had passed, so she merely answered her

aunt, 'that she was grieved to see her so ill, and
would do all she could to make her better.'
Her aunt then said something about sending for
her dead son, which showed Susan that she was
wandering again; and she gradually left the bed-
side, and seated herself quietly at her work, while
Mrs. Burnup talked in an under-tone to herself,
till she fell fast asleep.

When she awoke from this doze she appeared
more collected, and asked Susan how long she
had been ill, for she seemed in a dream. Susan
told her that it was a month since she first became so very ill. Her aunt looked almost in-
credulous, and asked why she did not come to
her sooner. Susan assured her that she went
to her the very first hour she was seized, but
Mrs. Burnup shook her head, and seemed distressed; so Susan begged her not to talk any
more just then, promising to tell her all about
it by and by, when she was stronger. For
several days she continued in the same state,
sometimes sensible, and at others wandering, but
constantly harping on the length of her illness,
and Susan not having come to her; for she
could not be persuaded, that she had been nursing
her from the commencement of her illness. At
length, one day, as she was gazing up at the
curtains of the bed, she seemed to be conscious,
for the first time, that she was not in her own
bed, and she asked Susan why they had taken it
from her, for like many persons in that complaint, she had become very suspicious. Susan

N

then told her, as quietly as she could, all that had happened; assuring her that her bed was safe at her own house; that she was at Susan's house, and being attended to, by her and little Margaret and Fanny. Poor Mrs. Burnup burst into tears at hearing this, saying, 'Then I am a burden to you, after all!' In vain Susan assured her, that it was the greatest pleasure to her, and her children to be of use to her. She would listen to nothing she said, but kept repeating alternately, 'Yes, a pretty expense to her—a heavy burden!' When she was silent, Susan told her that the expense was very little, compared to that which her brother had been to her aunt; 'and I can assure you, aunt,' said she, 'it is with such delight that he brings me every Saturday night half-a-crown from his earnings to be laid out for you.'

'But he does not come and see me,' said Mrs. Burnup. 'Why does he not come, that I may thank him?'

'He has only waited for you to ask for him, aunt; for he often comes to the house to inquire for you, and has peeped at you often when you were asleep.'

That evening Henry came to make his usual inquiries after his aunt, and was much pleased to find that she had been asking for him, and that he was to be allowed to see her. Susan gave him many injunctions about not showing his feelings, for fear of exciting his aunt, and he promised to follow her orders; but he was not so

well-trained as Susan, and when his aunt burst
into tears, and thanked him for all he was doing
for her, he wept like a child, and Susan could
only stop this weeping scene by scolding both
her brother and aunt, and threatening to turn
the former out of the room if he did not conduct
himself better. Henry understood the hint, and
wiping his eyes, soon turned the conversation to
other subjects.

Now that Mrs. Burnup understood all that
had happened, she seemed to be much more composed, and Susan then thought she might venture to propose my going in to see her, the first
time I called. The doctor told her that though
her aunt would probably never be materially
better, yet she might linger a long time, and
would most likely go off very suddenly at last.

It happened that, just as they were discussing
about whether they should send for me, or wait
till I might chance to pay them a visit, I called
to inquire why little Margaret was so often absent from school ; and I then found, that it was
in consequence of her mother requiring her to
wait on her aunt, when she herself was engaged
in washing, or anything else that occasioned her
to be in another room, as she did not like Mrs.
Burnup to be left alone. From that day to the
day of her death, which happened a twelvemonth
after, I was at Susan's cottage once or twice a
week, and had full opportunity of seeing her
exemplary patience, and cheerful submission, to a
trial which many would have thought a very

great hardship.   But she really seemed pleased
at being able to repay part of the debt which she
always considered she owed her aunt.   Well
would it be for all of us, if we bore in mind more
constantly than we do, the privations and troubles,
which our youthful years must have caused our
parents or relations ; for then, instead of letting
them end their days in a poor-house, amongst
those whom they care not for, and who care not
for them, we should see oftener than we do, the
old grandfather or grandmother at the family
table in our cottages, and thus receiving back, in
their old age, a portion of the care which, in
their younger days, they had bestowed upon their
children.   The only thing that used to distress
Susan was, to hear her aunt thank her for all
she was doing ; as she never could fancy that
she deserved it.   Her brother used to come regularly twice a week to see his aunt ; and though
her own two sons were settled a long way off,
they came twice to see her during her illness ; so
that the old lady had all the comfort which she
could have, whilst confined to her bed, which
continued for a whole year ; and then she calmly
and quietly slept away.

Though Susan had long expected the event,
yet she felt it very much.   The entire dependence of her aunt upon her for everything, had
made her, as it were, a child to her, and Susan
missed the hourly attention she had been used
to give her.   However, her confinement, shortly
after, gave her a charge requiring a care as con-

stant, and a pleasure still greater. She called the little girl who was born at this time after her aunt, whose name was Mary, and Simpson stood godfather to the little Christian.

My readers will know from this, that he had become a true churchman, though James at first had feared that all his arguments had been lost upon him, till a division among the Methodists took place, which opened Simpson's eyes to the truth of all that James had told him; and he became convinced that if once we leave the Church, we may go on and leave one sect after another, till we end in being Unitarians or infidels: we may divide and divide, till there is no religion left. And he often says, that he enjoys a tranquillity of mind and a calmness of devotion, when occupying his accustomed place in the church, which he never felt, in the excitement of going from one meeting-house to another.

CHAPTER XIII.

At this time, the illness of one of my own children obliged me to leave my parish for three months, to try what effect change of air would have upon her; having engaged a curate during the time of my absence. Before I left home, I

called to say good-bye to most of my flock; but
Susan and James begged to be allowed to come
and see us off; and though we did not leave till
eight o'clock, they were at the parsonage at
seven, assisting in cording boxes, &c., and it was
with tears in their eyes, and many a prayer for
the recovery of our little girl, that they bade us
farewell.

Poor James! little did we think, as we shook
him by the hand, that it was the last time we
should see him.   But it was even so.   Three
months after, when we visited Susan's cottage, it
was to see her arrayed in widow's weeds, and
her children fatherless!

My curate wrote me an account of his illness,
which was but of a week's continuance, caused
by inflammation, and terminating in brain fever.
He died insensible, and this, he said, added
greatly to Susan's distress, which he described
as being deeper than any he had ever witnessed,
but which, before we returned home, had assumed
a less excited character.   Yet it was melancholy
to see the change which grief had made in her
countenance, though it was blended with a mild
sweetness, which then took the place of her
former bright and laughing expression, and
which she retains to this day.

My curate told me that he was surprised to
see how, even in the midst of her griefs, she
strove to dwell on the mercies which had been
shown her in this heavy trial; and, as she dwelt
on the sorrow it caused her to think he was

unconscious of all that was said to him during the greater part of his illness, she would check herself by thinking that he was also insensible to much suffering, and that he was spared the pain of parting from them. One day, he told me, a neighbour came in and began to pity her for having so many children to provide for; but she checked her by turning to the curate, saying, ' These, sir, are my *blessings* in my trial ; *childless* widowhood would be very hard to bear; but my elder ones will soon help me to provide for the younger ones.'

It was a sad, sad visit, the first that my wife and I paid to our poor friend ; but it was one that we shall never forget. When tears would allow her to speak, there was something almost heavenly in the tone of her conversation; and she seemed to have pleasure in telling us how kind Simpson had been to her, and how often he expressed his thankfulness that James had shown him the sin of schism, and taught him to see the purity and truly Apostolic character of the Church. And though my curate happened *not* to be what is called a popular preacher, yet Simpson never thought of wandering from the Church.

My wife offered to take Margaret into our house, to bring her up as a nursery-maid, which offer Susan gladly accepted; and little Fanny remained with her mother until the baby could walk about; and then Susan placed her, at our recommendation, with a lady in the neighbourhood, to whom she has just become a valuable servant. Susan's brother has had the eldest boy bound apprentice to him; and the youngest is so fond of the sea, that poor Susan was obliged to let him be a sailor. Mary is now her only constant companion, and Susan has a little shop, which answers very well; for, being a great favourite with the ladies of the neighbourhood, they get all their stationery and nicknacks of her. It was in setting up this little shop that Susan found the advantage of their early prudence; for when James died, he had more than £200 in the Savings' Bank, and a portion of this, she laid out to stock her shop. Busily engaged in it I must now leave her. Often do I pay her a visit, and never do I leave her, without a feeling of thankfulness that she is still one of my flock.

At some future time I may tell my readers of the effects of her example, her advice, and her kindness, on the thoughtless, the misguided, and the afflicted, amongst her neighbours.

My present story has far exceeded its intended limits; but my labour will not have been in vain, if it excites one mother to greater care of her children; if it helps to reclaim one wandering son of the Church, or assists one humble member of it to understand its services and appreciate its usefulness.

SUSAN CARTER,

THE WIDOW.

𝔓art 𝔍𝔍𝔍.

––––––

CHAPTER I.

WHEN I last wrote of my old friend Susan
Dawes, I made a sort of half promise that I
would, at some future time, relate the effects
of her example and advice on some of her neighbours. This promise I have not been allowed
to forget, and the frequent inquiry of "When
are we to hear more of Susan?" has at last in-
duced me, to take up my pen once more in her
service. I must, however, begin by telling them,
that I fear to the younger part of them, at least,
she may not be considered quite so interesting a
person as when I had to tell of her in her orphan's
garb at the Asylum, as the favourite servant at
the Rectory, the wife of James, or the fond
mother of her first infant. So far she carried all
hearts with her, and perhaps still more so, when
I had to describe her, first, as the bereaved
mother, then as the sick and afflicted wife, and
lastly as arrayed in widow's weeds. I know
my young readers followed her in her prosperous

days with heartfelt pleasure, and at the relation of her latter sad ones, I am sure their kindly sympathy was not wanting. But now I can give them no promise of anything exciting. I will not even undertake to give an account of her life in regular course, from the time of her widowhood, for it is with her manner of thinking on various subjects connected with the practical duties of life, that I wish my readers to be acquainted. Of Susan personally I am sure I need not write, for they have known her long enough to fancy her in her shop, or little back room, the picture of neatness, with little Mary as her most willing, though very young, assistant. They must not fancy her with her former joyousness of spirit, neither must they imagine her dejected or downcast, for neither of these is her case. The widow's heart can never know the exuberance of overflowing happiness, nor can a mother, who is blessed in her children, indulge in useless and unavailing sorrow, I mean a widow and mother, such as my Susan, whose heart is stayed on God, and who loves to dwell on those comforting words of St. Paul, 'There remaineth *therefore* a rest *to* the people of God.'

Her most excited moments were, perhaps, when her sailor son threw his arms round her neck, after an absence of eighteen months, at the same moment pouring into her lap his hard-earned wages, and with all the warmth of an English sailor, and a Christian son, assuring her, that if he had worked doubly hard, he should feel more than repaid by the pleasure he then had, in sharing all he had with his mother : and then, like a genuine British tar, he would begin and 'wonder how any one could live always at home, for they never saw anything new, no new countries, no new faces, and never felt the joy of coming back again and knocking at their mother's door, and hearing her hurried step come to open it, and then rushing into her arms.' Poor Susan was often in tears as he dwelt on the delight of the sea, and would in vain try to argue him out of his notion, that no life was like a sailor's ; but she is now content to see him master of a little merchant vessel himself, and there setting an example to his crew of sobriety and industry founded on that Christian education given him by his mother, of fearing God and loving his Church. Yes, it is a pleasure to see him when he is at home for a few weeks, after a long absence, entering the church with her, his weather-beaten and manly face, contrasting finely with her pale, subdued countenance. It does my heart good to hear his deep-toned voice (shaming, alas ! many round him) joining in all the responses at church, to see him reverently kneeling at all the prayers, instead of lolling with his elbows on the pew, or lounging in one corner of it. But for this he was indebted to his mother. She taught him early in life how to conduct himself in the house of God, and when he was old, he 'did not depart from it.'

And now, my readers, before I go further, let me ask such of you as are parents, will *your* sons have to thank you for the same careful bringing up? Will they hereafter bear their part in all the services of the Church, because you have taught them to do so? You all, I know, admire Susan; but do you try to resemble her? It is not that you may *admire* her merely that I write, but that you may imitate her.

One man, who had read the former part of Susan's life, told me that 'I should have given it him sooner to read, and then he would have tried to have found a Susan.' Now although it is far from my wish to make husbands discontented with their choice, (for being once made they must abide by it), yet I am most anxious that those wives and mothers, who feel they are not acting their part as such like Susan, should at once endeavour to become like her. I will not tell them how this is to be done, because I hope some of Susan's conversations will throw a little light on that matter. Her little shop brings many people in her way, and her known kindness, in all cases of sickness and distress, makes her a general favourite; and when she offers her advice she has such a mild conciliating way of doing it, that even if she fails to convince, which is not often, she never offends. Often do I find, when any little cause of annoyance or dispute has arisen in the village, which they come to me to decide, when I have given my opinion, the rejoinder is, 'Well, sir, that's just what Susan Dawes said, but they would not be satisfied without coming to you, but I believe she is oftener right than wrong.' I cannot tell my readers of half the good she has done and is doing in my parish; and this may teach them, that it is not birth, nor fortune, nor high rank, that is requisite for obtaining influence.

Every one who has read Susan's little history must have learnt from it, that the orphan girl at the Asylum had influence over her schoolfellows; that the nursery maid at the Rectory had influence over her fellow-servants; that Susan Dawes, the wife of a groom, had influence over her neighbours; and they may believe my assurance, that this influence is increasing with her declining years. To what, then, you will ask, was this influence owing? Certainly not to birth, nor riches, nor high station. No, this latter kind of influence, can be possessed by *few*, but hers is within the reach of *all*. The true secret of her influence, was consistency of conduct, that is, a working out in ourselves those principles which we recommend to others. In vain shall we talk to them of holiness if we show it not in our lives. It is so *very* easy to talk, and, alas! so very difficult to practise; but we may rest assured that without the latter the former is worse than useless. There was no advice which Susan gave that her listener did not feel, 'Oh! yes, I am sure *you* would do so

and so,' or 'I know that is precisely what you
did under similar circumstances,' and thus her
advice made its way to the heart, and the understanding.   Let it not, however, be imagined that
Susan possessed the same kind of influence over
all.   Oh, no! It was on the well-disposed, and
often on the weak and wavering, that she had a
really beneficial effect, but on the wilfully neg-
ligent her influence was of another kind.   They
feared and avoided her.   Some of them respected
her, but others too often would sneeringly say,
'Well, I would not be as precise as Susan Dawes
for all the world!' though if a time of trouble
came upon them, they would afterwards find
that Susan was their best friend, and it was
often painful to her, to hear them lamenting most
bitterly, that they had ever spoken slightingly, or
disparagingly of her.

I was very much amused one day at hearing
of the plan she had pursued with a person who
lived a mile from the church, and who was apt
to allow the most trifling excuse to prevent her
attending on a Sunday.   It happened that she
had been drinking tea with Susan one Thursday,
and afterwards the conversation turned on the
difficulty of getting to church, as Hannah Lee
expressed it (for that was the name of Susan's
friend), when there was a hot dinner to be cooked.
Susan quickly proved to her the possibility
of having a hot dinner, and yet not being
obliged to stay at home to cook it, by prepar-

ing a pie the day before, or putting some broth on the fire which might be safely left to cook itself whilst she was at church. Hannah promised to make the attempt the following Sunday, Susan having assured her that it required nothing but a little management and forethought.

'Of course,' she said, 'you must get up a little sooner on Sundays, and ——' she was going on, but Hannah interrupted her by saying,

'Now, Mrs. Dawes, who could have told you that I did not get up soon on a Sunday?'

'Not any one, I assure you, Hannah, excepting yourself at this moment. I did not suppose that you did *not* get up early on a Sunday, but what I meant was, that if need be, you should get up a little earlier on a Sunday than on any other day, and I know you are not disposed to lie in bed on other mornings, for I have seen you go off to the fields by six o'clock.'

'Aye, aye, Mrs. Dawes, that's because I'm forced to it you see, and on Sunday it's more of a day to myself, and I think I may indulge myself a little.'

'Indeed! a day to yourself, Hannah! why, I thought it was the only day in the seven that was *not* our own, that we had six given us for our own work, but that the remaining one was specially *God's* day, and that in it we were *not* to do our own work, nor to seek our own pleasure, but that both in body and mind we were on that day to be entirely devoted to God's service.'

'Well, to be sure, the commandment does say so, but you see when one has a large family, and is hard at work all the week, it is only natural to take a little rest on a Sunday.'

'Yes, Hannah, it is quite natural, and not only natural but necessary, and God who knows what is necessary for us, has in His mercy provided that it shall be a day of rest for us; but the point is, in what does this rest consist? Not in lying in bed, I think, and then being in such a bustle to get the children ready for the national school and church, that you have no time to prepare either your mind or body for going there yourself, nor in preparing a hot dinner for your husband, which might have been done as easily the day before: this surely is not *rest*, Hannah?'

'Well but, Mrs. Dawes, you see that my husband does like a hot dinner on a Sunday; he says that he is obliged to get it cold all the week, or at least only half warmed (for you know I always send it to him at his work), and he thinks it is hard if he cannot have it one day in the week comfortably with his family.'

'Indeed I think so, too, Hannah. Sunday is a day of joyful thankfulness, and I would by all means have you make it one of comfort to your husband. It is not the hot dinner that I am speaking about, but it is your staying from church to cook it, and as I explained to you just now, you can put your pie in the oven, or your broth on the fire, and find them all ready for you on your return home ; depend upon it " where there's a will there's a way," and I strongly suspect your husband will feel far greater satisfaction in having you on his arm as he goes to church, than in leaving you at home to cook his dinner, and you may depend he will think you are *not* a bad manager to let him have a hot dinner although you had not been at home to look after it.'

'Well, I dare say you are right, Mrs. Dawes, (indeed I should be pleased if I could once catch you in the wrong,) for many a time he has said, " I wish you would let one of the bairns stay at home and mind the dinner whilst you come to church with me, for it does not seem right that you should always be the one to stay at home ;" but somehow or other I've put him off from Sunday to Sunday till now he's left off asking me, but I'll give him a surprise before long.'

'Mind you do, Hannah, and don't let any little silly excuse stop you. I shall look for you next Sunday as I come out of church, so don't disappoint me. Mind and be up in time.'

'Oh! never fear, I'll be up with the lark, I promise. By the by, do you think you'll be going to the market on Saturday, for I want to buy some bits of things for the bairns, and I should like your opinion on them ?'

'I cannot go next Saturday, Hannah, but the

o

Saturday after I must go; for I want to meet Fanny, who is coming home for a day or two.'

'Will you go in the morning, or afternoon, do you think?'

'Why I am not quite certain, but most likely it will be after one, and I will just run up and call for you.'

'Oh! but that would be taking you out of your way.'

'Never mind, it will not make ten minutes' difference, for we can take the short cut from your house.'

'Well, thank you, thank you, good bye, I've stayed gossiping longer than I intended, but it has not been a bad gossip, has it?'

'I hope not,' said Susan, 'but Sunday will show whether it has been *good* or not.'

The next Sunday Hannah Lee's husband joined Susan in the churchyard after service. He saw she was looking round to see if his wife was there, so before she had time to ask any questions, he said,

'Ah! I know you're wondering why my mistress is not here, but it's not from lying over-late this time, I can tell you, but you see it was damp and looked so like rain, that she was afraid of coming, and you see it's raining fast now, so may be it's as well she didn't come, or it might have frightened her against another Sunday.'

'Well, really, William, I differ from you, for

if she had but come she would have found that
with her old cloak she would have taken no harm,
especially as she would have had you to hold the
umbrella over her.'

'Well, to be sure, that's true, but you see
she's a little frightened about herself or her
clothes (he added, laughing), and I had sore
work to get her to let the children go with me
this morning, but I've no notion of bringing
them up to think that a drop of rain is to stop
them from coming to church; and I must say
they have no wish to do so neither, for it's a dull
day to them when they have to stop in the house
all the day, and that I make them do if they are
not at church, for it won't do to let them find an
excuse for staying from God's house, and then go
wandering half over the country with all the idle
vagabonds they may meet with : but, as I said
before, they've no inclination for it, but they
look to coming to church morning and evening
just as natural as they look for their dinner.
"Use is second nature," the old proverb says,
and so I like to use them to good habits, and
that will keep them out of bad ones.'

'Ah! William, it is very true,' said Susan;
'I believe the proper observance of the Lord's
day, brings with it greater blessings than either
you or I are aware of, and certainly we know
that many curses have followed the breaking it;
and if it was only for the inward peace and content which it brings with it, I think one might

very truly say, that this commandment is not
" grievous." '

'I am sure I can say so, Mrs. Dawes; and if
I could but get my mistress to think so too, I
believe there would be few happier families on a
Sunday.'

'Have patience, William; you know the old
proverb which you mentioned just now, and
remember that unluckily her " use " has been in
the wrong way, and it will take time to bring her
into the right one. Tell her that I am sorry to find
she is so delicate as to be afraid of a little rain.'

William laughed, saying, ' Oh! I assure you
she's as strong as I am every bit.'

' Well, well, never mind, give her my message,'
said Susan, smiling, whilst little Mary looked up
in her face and said,

' I'm sure, mother, Hannah looks far stouter
than you do, and has a deal more colour; I don't
think that she can be weakly.'

' It is not always the stoutest-looking, Mary,
that are the strongest,' said her mother, ' nor can
they always stand as much hardship, as many
who are pale and thin.'

' I'm sure, mother,' said Mary, ' you are pale
and thin enough, and yet you can do a great deal,
and I never saw you kept from church by the
weather.'

' We are nearer than Hannah Lee you know,
dear, and though I am pale and thin now, yet
God is so good as to give me strength for all I

have to do; and He gave me you too, my Mary, who do help me as much as your strength will allow you, and I'm sure will help me more if God spares you life and health.'

'I hope so, my dear mother, for I do feel so happy when I think I can be of use to you, and when I see you tired I do so wish that I was older and could help you more.'

'All in good time, Mary; it is a comfort to me to see you trying to help me, and I daily thank God for having given me so kind and thoughtful a little girl.'

By this time they had reached their own door, and Mary presently got out the dinner things, and they had as comfortable a dinner (and certainly a cleaner one) than many of those who had stayed from church that morning. Indeed, as my readers will guess from what they know of Susan, she did not allow Mary to spend her time on Sunday in doing anything which could be as well done on the following day; so the few plates and dishes were put aside in a cupboard, and the room was still the picture of neatness and cleanliness. Sometimes on a Sunday evening she and Mary had the pleasure of a visit from Margaret on her way from evening service; for Susan kept to her old practice of going to church in the morning and afternoon, and staying at home in the evening, when Mary and she would read about the services of the day, or talk over anything which had particularly attracted their attention

in the sermon, and this in that spirit of affectionate reverence with which everything belonging to
the Church and its ministers should always be
handled. Sometimes Susan would describe to
Mary, the delight her good father had in hearing
her brothers and sisters say their hymns and
catechism, and read a chapter or two in the
Bible on the Sunday evening ; and she would tell
her how pleased he would have been had he lived
to see his little Mary reading also. And then little
Mary's eyes would fill with tears when she heard
about her father, whom, alas ! she had never
known ; but Susan would then begin and talk
to her of the great blessing it was to both of
them that they could remain together : and
Mary's little heart would be so full that she
could with difficulty say, 'Yes, God has given
me a dear good mother, and I do thank Him for
that.'

Poor Susan ! her tears, she would often say,
were not bitter ones. She loved to dwell on the
recollection of her husband's good qualities. As
a husband, as a father, and as a consistent,
upright Christian, sincerely attached to the
Church, she thought she had never seen his equal,
and her daily prayer was that she might be fitted
to rejoin him hereafter. She did not wish to
drive the thought of his loss from her, she felt
truly that with her 'the memory of the just'
was 'blessed,' but she still wished to feel that it
was a trial sent for her good, sent to wean her

from this world, and which must almost insens-
ibly draw her thoughts to another. She felt
as if it must be a greater sin in her to be
wedded to this world when her strongest tie was
gone, than it was in those who had all their earthly ties unbroken; but she also felt too that the
beautiful portion of our creed which says 'I
believe in the communion of saints,' breathed a
comfort and joy to her which those only could
feel who were separated in body, but not in spirit,
from those who, they truly hoped, had joined the
saints in the unseen world.

But I must return to Hannah Lee; for the
following Saturday she expected Susan to call for
her to go to the market, but no, Susan did not
appear, and Hannah in despair set off without
her. The fact was, the day was extremely wet,
not merely showers as it had been the previous
Sunday, but a continued rain, so of course Susan
concluded, that if she could not walk one mile to
church on a showery day, she could not walk
three to town when it was raining unceasingly.
Susan, however, had been mistaken, and Hannah
went to town an hour or two after she herself
had set off. In the evening, as she returned, she
called at Susan's, saying,

'Well, Mrs. Dawes, I suppose you have not
been at the town to-day?'

Susan stared as she saw her standing drenched
with rain, and begged her to go home and change
her clothes immediately, and she would tell her

at some other time whether she had been to town or not, for she knew that if she said she had, it would lead to a long parley; so she gave Hannah a dry umbrella, telling her she could get her own the next day either on her road to or from church. Sunday proved a beautiful day, and before Susan had seated herself, she had the pleasure of seeing William Lee walk up the aisle with his wife. It happened that the holy Communion was administered that day, and as, I am sorry to say, neither William nor Hannah at this time approached the Lord's table, Susan saw nothing of them until after the service in the afternoon. Before they were fairly out of the churchyard gates, however, Hannah seized hold of Susan's arm, saying,

'Now, I know you were in town yesterday, though you would not say so last night.'

'Yes, I was,' said Susan, 'for, though I thought Fanny's mistress would not let her come away in the rain (for you know she is but delicate), I did not like to run the risk of her being in town and I not there to meet her; but of course I never thought of your going, Hannah, as I knew your business was of no great consequence, and as a shower frightened you from taking a *short* walk to church last Sunday I was pretty sure you would not choose a *long* walk in pouring rain.'

'Oh! but you see, Mrs. Dawes, I had already put off two Saturdays; last Saturday you know

you could not go with me, and the week before
my husband wanted me to help him in the garden,
and I began to think that if I allowed one thing
after another to put me off, the poor bairns
would never get their frocks, so I made up my
mind to face the weather, and you see I am none
the worse for it.'

At this, William, who had scarcely kept down
a smile during the greater part of this sentence,
burst into a loud laugh, for he saw what Susan
was aiming at, but Hannah did not see her drift,
and rather impatiently asked her husband what
he was laughing at.   He merely replied,

'Oh ! Mrs. Dawes will tell you presently.'

'Indeed !' said Hannah, 'I thought you were
laughing because I said I was none the worse for
my wetting, and I'm sure I am not.'

'No,' said Susan, 'you do not indeed appear
to be so, and I was just thinking that if you
could stand such a complete drenching without
harm, you were not quite so delicate as I feared
last Sunday that you might be.'

'Nay, nay, Mrs. Dawes, you never thought
that, I'm sure.'

'Then why were you afraid of a shower of
rain ?'

'Why, you know it was not for *myself* that I
was frightened, but one does not like to get one's
best clothes spoilt in one Sunday, for it's hard
enough work to get them, and yet one does like
to be *decent* at church.'

'Oh! certainly,' said Susan, 'but on a wet day I should not think of putting on my best stuff gown nor my best shawl, but I should put on my old one and my great wrapping cloak, which I take off in church, and yet I hope I am decent, Hannah.'

'Oh! well, to be sure, I had not thought of that.'

'And yet I suppose you put on all your old things yesterday, though in a general way I suspect you like to make yourself *decent* when you go to the town.'

'Why, yes, to be sure I did, for I felt that I must go, and that it was no use putting off and putting off.'

'But with respect to church, then, you don't mind putting off Sunday after Sunday; you had been twice prevented going to market, I wonder how many times you have been prevented coming to church.'

'Oh! twenty times that number, I dare say,' said Hannah, who was now beginning to see that Susan would soon convict her out of her own mouth; 'but then you see it was downright necessaries that I wanted from the town.'

'Downright necessaries for the body, Hannah, I dare say, and mind I don't blame you for going in the rain to get them, but have you then no downright necessaries for the soul to seek at church, no sins to confess, no pardon to pray for, no blessings to ask, no thanks to render, no belief to declare in your God and Saviour, no love to profess for His Holy Church, and no instruction to receive? Are all these things *unnecessary*? If your children's bodies and your own cannot subsist without food or raiment, do you think your soul can be supported without spiritual food?'

'Well, but, Mrs. Dawes, don't you think I can find spiritual food when I am hindered from getting to church?'

'Certainly you may, but in a much less degree than you do at church; but then the question always comes, *do* you get it at home, and if it is wilfully that we neglect the "assembling of ourselves together," as God has commanded us, in His holy temple, are we likely, think you, to have His blessing on our prayers and readings at home? You know that I am a plain-spoken person, and I know that you are good-tempered and will not allow what I say in sincerity to offend you, so just let me ask how much of last Sunday *was* really employed by you, whilst your husband and children were at church, in prayer? Let me ask you, if you have no objection, that plain question.'

Hannah looked confused, and said, 'Ah! Mrs. Dawes, I see that you know me far better than I know myself, for I'm sure, though you ask the question, you know that I did not open my Prayer-Book.'

'No, indeed, I knew no such thing, but I

know perfectly well that we are all apt to say,
" Oh ! we can pray at home," when we ought to
go to church to pray, whereas the truth of the
matter is, the people who neglect to go to church
are just the people who do *not* pray at home ; it
is only an excuse which Satan puts into our
hearts, for he knows very well, that if he once
gets us to neglect those means of grace which
God has given us, he will have us more and more
in his power. He knows that the sight of the
church and the hearing of God's minister calling
on us to confess our sins must rouse us to think
of our manifold transgressions and to repent of
them ; whilst the declaration also by the minister
of God's mercy, and that he " willeth not the
death of a sinner," must lead us to rely on
Christ's atonement for forgiveness. Satan knows
that, whilst we are making use of the ordinances
of Christ's Church, we are drawn near to Christ,
and that so his own power over us will grow
weaker and weaker ; but he knows that no sooner
does he get us to renounce these than we are his,
at least for a time. I dare say, Hannah, your feelings and thoughts this morning in church were
very different from what they were last Sunday
in your own house ? '

' Yes, that they were ; for of course at home I
was thinking only of the dinner, and dusting some
things which I had slighted before breakfast, and
then I sat watching the weather and wondering
whether William and the bairns would get wet.'

'So you see, Hannah, that though you had *time* for praying, it seems you did not think of that : but I'll say no more, I dare say you think I've given you a long enough lecture for one day, and I must say you've taken it well.'

'Why, I don't know how one could take anything ill from you, Mrs. Dawes ; I wish I only saw things always as you do, and I'll try to think of what you've said to-day, and not be absent from church for bad weather again.'

'No,' said Susan, 'nor for any other petty excuse ; my dear husband used to say that his good master had said to him when a lad and he had made some poor excuse for not attending church, " Now, James, don't deceive yourself or me, for you know you cannot deceive God ; but just ask yourself whether you would have thought this a sufficient reason for your not joining a party of pleasure, and if you would not, be sure that it is the deceitfulness of your heart which makes you *fancy* that it is a reason why you should not go to church." '

'Ay, ay,' said William, who had been listening very attentively to all that had been said, ' if Hannah just asks herself whether such and such a thing could keep her from the *market*, I suspect the answer will be oftener in favour of the church than against it ; but we have passed your door with our chat, Mrs. Dawes, so supposing you come and drink tea with us ? "

' Not to-night, thank you, I may see Margaret

in the evening, and perhaps my boy James may be coming over to tea.'

They bid good bye to each other, and all the way home William and Hannah could talk of nothing but Susan's good sense, and her right way of looking at things, and her kindness of heart ; and they both felt a desire to grow more and more like her, wishing it had happened that they had sooner become intimate with her.

CHAPTER II.

AMONGST the many people to whom Susan had been of benefit in the village, was a woman of the name of Carmichael. She was a married woman without children, and at the time of the death of her mother (who had lived with her and her husband), Susan was the only person who, in the scene of suffering that was going forward, never lost her presence of mind, and who was able by her kind thoughtfulness to administer relief when others flew from the bed-side at the sound of groans almost too terrible to think of. Her daughter could not remain even in the same house with her ; and of those neighbours who came in nominally to lend assistance, the greater part stood talking about the horror of the poor woman's state instead of trying to relieve the sufferer; and when the poor woman breathed her last, Susan was the only one who stood by the bed-side, as pale, indeed, almost as the corpse before her, but with a countenance that seemed to say, 'If we forsake the dying, how can we expect to have our own death-bed soothed by tenderness and attention?' Her husband, James Carmichael, was a hard-labouring man, and lived quietly enough with his wife, excepting when he occasionally broke out into a drunken fit, which never lasted long, and which he seemed to think did no one any harm but himself; for as he had no children he thought the money would not be much missed. He generally went to church once a day on Sunday, and used to grumble at his wife because she would not always go with him, but would run after some preacher at the Methodist, Ranter, or Independent meeting. It was useless his telling her that he had been brought up to the Church, and would keep to it, for she always retorted on him by asking him ' if the Church told him to get drunk?' adding, that, if the church ministers could not cure him of drinking, their sermons were not worth much. Susan happened to mention this couple to me, and I took an opportunity of looking into their cottage one day as I was passing. Carmichael was sitting reading the Bible as I entered, and his wife was preparing tea.

He smiled as I went in, saying he had been

wishing to see me for many a day, 'for,' said
he, 'my wife and I cannot agree on one or two
points, and though she has been to Mrs. Dawes,
who is on my side in the matter, Margery is not
content, but keeps on with her old ways ; but if
you are on my side, sir, and I think you will be
(he added smiling), there may be better hopes for
me.'   I could not help smiling too, and said
that of course it must depend upon whether it
was a subject for me to settle, and next, whether
his wife would abide by my decision.

Margery coloured up, saying, that 'Carmichael was fond of making a noise about nothing,
and that for her part she thought she was old
enough to judge for herself, and that if. Mrs.
Dawes, who, she thought, was the most consistent person she knew, could not convince her,
she thought no one else could.'

'Well, Mrs. Carmichael,' said I, 'there are
few people whose principles and practice agree
more thoroughly than, I believe, hers do, and I
doubt not that she is as likely as any one to
make you think rightly ; but do let me hear what
is the knotty question now to be decided.'

'Why, sir,' said Carmichael (scratching his
head as if that was the weak part), 'the thing
is this.   You know, sir, that I always attend the
church, and have done so, sir, from a child, and
my wife here will go off to some one or other of
these meetings, just wherever there is the newest preacher, and she won't go to church, sir,

because, she says, she does not think your sermons can be good for much because——' poor Margery tried to stop him, but it was of no use, and he went on, appearing half ashamed of himself, 'because, sir, I sometimes get more beer than I ought. I know it's wrong in me, sir, but I think it's worse in her to blame you for it, and to keep from the church for my fault.'

I really could not help laughing at an idea which was new to me, that my sermons were considered useless because there was one man whom they did not cure of drunkenness, and I turned round to Margery, and said, 'Then a drunken fit is unknown amongst all the men who attend these various meeting-houses I suppose, Mrs. Carmichael?'

'Ah! but she cannot say that though,' said her husband, 'for I could tell you of a dozen that are drunk twelve times to my once, sir; for after all, Mr. Wilson, I'm not a *very* out-of-the-way man, even Margery can't say that I am,—can you now, mistress?'

'Oh! you're well enough as times go,' said she, 'excepting now and then, but you know, sir, he wants to make out that the Church is above all other religions, and so I just teaze him by saying it hasn't made him above other men in the matter of drink, but it's as much as anything to plague him a bit, that he mayn't be so hard on the Methodists and the rest of the folks of a different persuasion.'

'Well, my good woman,' I replied, 'you are

r

a very odd reasoner, indeed ; you think to make him less hard on others, by being yourself very hard on him and me,—and as you seem to judge of the teaching of the Church by the practice of its members (or *nominal* members), of course you won't object to my judging of dissenting teaching by dissenting practice,—you can't say that I am hard upon you in doing so. Come, Mrs. Carmichael,' I said, seeing she knew not what to say, ' do we agree so far ? '

Margery looked confused, and said it was not fair of her husband to take her so by surprise, and to go and tell me all that she had said.

' Oh ! then you feel,' said I, ' that you have no just ground for refusing to go to church with your husband : if you admit this I dare say he will be satisfied, and I won't weary you with arguments in favour of your doing so from the fact of your having been baptized, confirmed, and married in it.'

' As to that, sir, I must say Mrs. Dawes has told me all that, and certainly when I hear her talk, and still more, as I said before, when I see her practice, I do feel she is right in most things, though I think both she and my husband are rather bigoted.'

' And what do you mean by being bigoted ? ' I asked.

' Why, they fancy the Church is the right way, and won't hear of any other ; and then I can't think it is the only right way, because I see so many bad people belong to it. If all the folks that are church-goers were like Susan Dawes, I own I should have a better notion of the Church.'

'Then you find all dissenters good people, do you? at least as far as you are capable of judging, for after all it is God only who knows who are good. You have never met with any one amongst them, who fancied that their sect only could be saved? You never met with a liar, a drunkard, or, in short, you never have seen anything but what you admire in the dissenters of all kinds with whom you associate in worship?'

'Ay,' said Carmichael, in ecstasy at all these home questions, 'just answer the Rector according as you have found them, that's all.'

'Come, my friend,' said I, 'give your wife time for reflection; she is not so apt at seeing faults perhaps as you are.'

'Oh! but you can see mine; can't you, Margery?'

'And I dare say the clergyman can see them too, or he is not very far-sighted,' retorted the wife.

'Well,' said I, 'this is not the way to come to the point that you and I are talking about, Mrs. Carmichael. I have something to say to your husband, but in the mean time I should like to have an answer to my question.'

Margery coloured and stammered, and knew not what to say, for she was aware that her husband knew of several cases of drunkenness, cheating, and lying which had lately taken place, so she quietly said, that 'no doubt they had their faults as well as other folks.'

'I have no doubt they have,' I replied, 'and therefore let me beg of you in fairness not to bring against the Church what may be brought equally against dissent, namely, the inconsistent conduct of its members. Judge of the effect of the principles of the Church by looking at the life of a person who really follows the teaching of the Church, who reads, marks, learns, and inwardly digests the Holy Scriptures, and who takes the Book of Common Prayer, which is the Church's practical guide to all its members, in his hand, and seeks every day to live accordingly.'

A slight pause ensued. Mrs. Carmichael seemed to be considering what she had to say; at last she resumed, by saying, 'Well, as I said before, Susan Dawes is a real good churchwoman, and a real good Christian too; at least, I have never seen one of any sect who seemed to me as good as she is. I would rather be like Susan Dawes than any one of your parishioners, Mr. Wilson, not excepting great Lady Noakes herself; but it would be a hard job for me to be like her, sir.'

'Why, certainly,' said I, 'the way you have been going on is not exactly Mrs. Dawes's way. You have been running after this preacher and that, and not even within the pale of the Church. It is not right for people to go running from church to church, neglecting their own parish

church, the place where, above all others, they
may expect God's blessing to attend them; but
still in the Church you are sure of having the
same creeds and the same prayers, the same
"form of sound words," and the Sacraments duly
administered; but in going from one meeting-
house to another you have no creed, no form of
prayer; and you rely on the authority, or, it
may be, the mere imagination, of one man, for
what you are to pray for, what to be thankful
for, and what you are to praise God for.'

'Well, sir,' said Margery, 'I think there is
some truth in that; for though I like to hear
their sermons now and then, I don't fancy them
for anything else, for you know I was always
used to the Church from a child; but then, you
see, sir, Carmichael does not take the Sacrament,
though he does attend the Church, so I am no
worse than he is, after all; and I am sure the
sermons are often very affecting. Last Sunday
my handkerchief was right dripping, I cried
so.'

'Indeed?' said I; and I paused, thinking
she would go on to relate the effect of her tears:
but finding she did not, I inquired 'what good
her tears had done her? Had they led her to
search her heart more thoroughly; to examine
her thoughts more closely; to watch her daily
conduct more narrowly; to be more earnest in
seeking after the will of her Lord and Master,
and in striving to follow it?' Margery looked
confounded at these questions. She had certain-

ly, she thought, 'felt very near Christ' when
Mr. Thompson was preaching; she had 'felt a
burning love to Him,' and she wished she could
retain that feeling; but somehow or other, she
could not but own that it left her afterwards she
knew not how.

'Why I fear, Mrs. Carmichael,' said I, 'that
these violently excited feelings seldom leave any
lasting impression behind them. You seem to
think this yourself, and yet you go on Sunday
after Sunday having your ears tickled and feelings excited, and think that you are doing your
duty, while you refuse to come to the calm and
sober service of the Church, to confess your sins, to
receive thereupon the declaration of God's forgiveness by His Minister through Jesus Christ; to
hear God's word read to you in such regular order,
that, if you are not wanting in your attendance,
all the most instructive parts of the Old Testament, and all the history of our Saviour and
His doctrines, are brought in order before you
by the Church, who leaves not any of the truths
of the Gospel to the choice of her ministers as
to *when* they should teach them, but appoints
certain days, when she herself teaches all her
members.'

'How do you mean, sir?' said Margery, quite
astonished. 'How does the Church teach
us?'

'By her Prayer-book, which she requires all
her ministers to conform to; and in this Prayer-
book she appoints certain days for commemorat-

ing certain events. For instance, the Church year commences with Advent, to prepare us for Christmas, when we commemorate Christ's birth. Then comes His Circumcision, His Manifestation to the Gentiles, till we have celebrated all the leading events of His life. Then, after celebrating His Crucifixion, Resurrection, and Ascension, we commemorate the descent of the Holy Ghost the Comforter ; and the following Sunday is devoted to acknowledging the glory of the eternal Trinity. Now I do not hesitate to say that if the Church had not thus wisely provided a liturgy for us, to tell us not only *what* to pray for, but *when* we are to do so, and had left it to the choice of her ministers what portions of Scripture should be read in church, it is very possible that every congregation would have to lament the absence of some important doctrine, or forgetfulness of some historical fact, which now at stated seasons of the year they have brought before them.'

'Well,' said Margery, apparently occupied with thoughts which were new to her, ' I never looked at the Church and dissenters in that way before ; and certainly the dissenters do not like to observe days, though they might preach on all these different things too, if they thought of it : yet they do say a great deal about Christ being crucified for us, and His great love for us ; and they do beg us to come to Him.'

'Your account,' said I, 'is a specimen of a sermon full of exhortation and declamation, but wanting that plain and simple instruction, both in doctrine and practice, which is necessary to form a sincere Christian. It is not excited feelings which will make us Christ's disciples: it is a daily self-denying walking with Him in our ordinary calling,—doing this thing, and avoiding that, because Christ has forbidden or commanded it.'

Margery looked very grave: she seemed to say, by her looks, that it was a more serious subject than she had thought; and, as I feared to destroy the impression which appeared to have been made, I turned to her husband, who appeared to be scarcely less attentive, and said to him—' Well, Carmichael, I think a little consideration will make your wife see the duty of her attending church in a different light from that which she does at present; but I have a word or two for you before I leave. If you wish your wife to become a consistent churchwoman, you must let her see the teaching of the Church shown forth in your own life. You must become yourself more than a churchman in name: you must remember your baptismal vows, and act up to them. You must not fancy that attending church once on a Sunday is all that is required of you. You must endeavour to attend every service of the Church, and you must try to show, in your daily conduct, that you practise those duties which you have there been taught out of God's word.'

'Ay,' said Carmichael, 'I dare say I have been as much to blame as my wife, and we must both turn over a new leaf. I knew you would set us all to rights, sir.'

'Why, as to that, my friend, it is not a work of a moment to turn from evil to good. We cannot leave off bad habits, and acquire good ones, without many painful struggles, and perhaps even some sad relapses. A good resolution is one step, but before reformation comes, there must be many others—sincere repentance, earnest prayer to God, a hearty desire and striving to do His will, and a humble dependence on His Holy Spirit for assistance in the work; but do not for one moment fancy, Carmichael, that because all these are necessary, the work is too hard for you to set about; nor, on the other hand, be discouraged if your present warm feelings for the Church should become less ardent, or if your wife should again be " halting between two opinions." It must be God's grace alone, which will lead you both into all truth.'

'Well, thank you, sir, thank you, for all your good advice; I'm sure I hope that we shall not forget it, and if you'll look in some other day we'll be thankful to see you.'

I had heard enough of Margery Carmichael from Susan, not to allow my hopes to be raised very high about the real effect of the late conversation on her practice. She was evidently surprised at what I had told her, and apparently convinced; but how she would stand the next temptation was still a matter of doubt. Of James I had better hopes. He was a plain

matter-of-fact person, and if he were but convinced, he would not easily be drawn aside.
By some means or other he got Margery to
church with him the following Sunday, and for
several Sundays after (as I learned from Susan),
and she began to hope that there was more
firmness and steadiness in her character, than
she had before fancied; when her hopes were
again dashed to the ground. Perhaps some of
my readers will wonder, when I tell them how
Margery was drawn from the church for another
Sunday, for I believe it was the last time of her
being so.   It was the announcement that a
female was to take Mr. Thompson's pulpit on
the next Sunday, and would 'engage in prayer,'
and afterwards ' address her hearers ' on some
interesting subject.   Such, as far as I can remember, was the tenor of the bill put out on the
occasion (for when I returned home, the lamp-
posts and walls were still disgraced with notices
of this most unbecoming exhibition), and this
was the bait which once more drew Margery
aside from the right path.   In the morning she
accompanied her husband to church, but in the
afternoon she was in a greater hurry than usual
to put on her bonnet; and upon Carmichael's
inquiring why she was in such haste, she replied
that Mary Parker was going to call for her, to
go and hear Betsy Newtongue preach.   Her
husband stared, and was very near growing
warm, when he remembered what I had said to
him, and he merely said, ' Are you doing right,

think you, wife, in encouraging any woman to make a show of herself in this manner ? '

' Oh ! as to that,' said Margery, ' I don't see there's any very great harm in it. I have no doubt it will be very amusing.'

' Oh ! ' said her husband, calmly, ' if you are going to a place of worship to be amused, that is another business indeed. I hope, wife, when you get there you will just ask yourself, whether that is the way to worship God.'

Margery had no time for a reply, for Mary Parker was at the door, and away they went together, Mrs. Carmichael saying, ' Well, good afternoon, Carmichael ; I'll be in to tea ! ' Carmichael made no reply, but seated himself down to look over the second lesson for the afternoon. It happened to be the third chapter of the Second Epistle to Timothy. When he came to the sixth and seventh verses he suddenly stopped, and repeated, over and over again, the seventh verse : ' Ever learning, and never able to come to the knowledge of the truth.' ' Well,' said he, ' I hope that's not my poor wife's case.' But he was roused from his meditations by the sound of the ' church-going bell,' when, taking his Prayer-book in his hand, he set out for church. On the road, whom should he fall in with but Mrs. Dawes ? Somehow or other he felt that he would rather have avoided meeting her that day, though generally he was pleased to do so ; but he knew that her first question would be, ' Where is your wife this afternoon ? ' and he

was ashamed to tell her. However, Susan joined him, and, as he had anticipated, inquired
after Margery.

' She's not coming to church this afternoon,'
he replied.

' I hope she is not ill,' said Susan.

' Oh ! no, not ill, but she's gone with a neighbour.'

He said no more, and Susan did not curiously
inquire, thinking it most probable that she had
gone to see some sick friend. She saw, too, that
Carmichael was not in his usual spirits, and she
said very little to him. When service was over
he sauntered about the churchyard, and waited
till all the congregation had dispersed before he
went home, as he wished to avoid company on
the road. His own thoughts oppressed him
very much ; not only as to his wife's absence
from church, but he could not help feeling that
his former inconsistent conduct had, perhaps,
helped to make her inconsistent. ' Yes,' thought
he, ' I used not to attend church on Sunday
afternoon myself, so now my wife, perhaps,
thinks there's no more harm in her going to
this shameful sort of show, than in my strolling
about the fields, as I used to do. Well, I'll not
be hard upon her for it; but I pray God may
open her eyes to the error of her ways, as He
has done mine to the sinfulness of my own.'

When he reached home the kettle was boiling
on the hob, all ready for tea ; but though he had
lingered on the road, Margery had not arrived

before him. He sat down for a few minutes, still occupied by his former thoughts, till the church clock chimed the half-hour. He started up; could it be half-past five? He looked at his watch, and found it was so indeed. Then he went to the closet, took out the tea-things, setting a cup for his wife, who, he thought, would be in every minute. He waited for her till six —no Margery came, and he sat down to his solitary tea, reading his Bible during the time. Finding that she did not arrive, he began to fear that the address in the evening was the cause of her absence (as in truth it was), and he determined to sit down quietly to his Sunday evening reading, and try and prepare himself, fretful and uneasy as he was, for receiving her mildly on her return.

About nine o'clock, just as he had taken out the bread and cheese for his supper, Margery arrived. A large party had accompanied her home, but they did not come in. Carmichael heard them say, on taking leave of her, 'Now don't you believe all that the clergyman, and your husband, and Mrs. Dawes say about the Church; but just come and have a day with us when there's anything stirring going on, and we'll see if we can't get you converted yet.'

Poor Margery! she could make no reply. She tried to think that she had not done wrong, but yet did not feel any strong desire to go very soon again to hear this 'Betsy;' so she merely said, 'Good night.' When she entered, she expected her husband would have been angry with her, and was surprised at his quiet and subdued manner.

'Well, Margery,' he said, 'you see I've got supper ready for you. I waited tea for you a good while, but you have not kept me waiting a second meal.'

'Oh!' said she, 'Mary Parker would have me get tea with her, because she said she was sure you'd be keeping me at home in the evening, and as the 'Address' was to be about Temperance, I thought I might hear something to do you good, dear.'

Carmichael was again beginning to feel very angry, but happily checked himself, only saying, 'I'm sorry that you went on my account; we had a sermon this afternoon, from the Curate, on keeping our baptismal vows; and showing us that if we kept them, there was no need of any others. What have you been hearing about?'

'Why, Betsy Newtongue did not say anything about baptism: but she told us how easy it was to sign the book, and how much more healthy to drink water, and how much money we should save by not buying beer, and she told so many stories of people she had known who had grown quite rich, by just putting by the money they had formerly spent in drink. Some of the stories were really very pretty; I almost wish you could have heard them.'

'I cannot say that I have any wish to have been there. Our Curate said a good deal about temperance, but he did not make it out to be so easy to abstain from intemperance at all times, nor did he tell us that we were to do so just from worldly motives. He said that indulging in intemperance was contrary to God's word ; that it was a breaking of those vows which our godfathers and godmothers made for us in our baptism, and which we took on ourselves when we were confirmed ; then he spoke of the advantages of all acts of self-denial, and, especially, when by denying ourselves anything, it enabled us to assist the poor. "Yes," he said, "who would compare the momentary gratification of gluttony and drunkenness, (to say nothing of their attendant evils,) with the lasting pleasure of relieving the wants of our fellow-creatures, by denying our own palate, or refraining from indulgences of any kind?" There was nothing about growing rich by self-denial, wife.'

'Well, but, Carmichael,' said Margery, rather tartly, 'you don't expect Betsy Newtongue to preach like Mr. Barclay, who has had a college education, and knows Greek and Latin, and I don't know what else.'

'No, I certainly do not,' said he : 'I should expect to hear just such false reasoning brought forward as you mention. Instead of taking the only right ground in everything, of doing our duty because God commands us, she merely talks of worldly advantages. Surely you cannot think that this is the way to make a Christian. Our Lord said nothing like this. But it is useless beginning such a long subject as this so late at night ; but when you lay your head on your pillow, just recollect, that if Betsy is proved to be wrong on such a simple matter as drunkenness, how fearful must be her blunders if she presumes " to address her hearers," as it is called, on the mysteries of the Gospel ! '

Margery said she thought that was very likely —but she had worked a wonder to-day: for Sally Jenkins, who never would enter a place of worship before, declared she had felt her sins fall off that afternoon as Betsy was preaching. —' I'm sure Susan Dawes will be pleased to hear that she has been converted at last, though even by Betsy Newtongue.'

' I doubt it,' said Carmichael, 'but we'll go and see her to-morrow evening and hear all she has to say about it.'

' I shall be in for a lecture, that's certain,' said Margery, ' but she is so good herself that I can take her lectures quietly.'

They then got their supper, and Carmichael proposed afterwards to have prayers, which, by Susan Dawes' advice, they had had for the last month. James always concluded their Sunday evening prayer, after saying the confession, one or two collects, and the Lord's prayer, with that beautiful prayer for Unity in the service appointed for the 20th day of June. When prayers were over, Carmichael saw that his wife had not that self-sufficiency and complacency about her which she had formerly had when she returned from the meeting. The following evening after tea, Carmichael proposed that they should go and visit Susan, according to their agreement. Margery willingly agreed, and off they set. Carmichael told her as they were going that he had seen Susan as he went to church on Sunday afternoon; and that she had inquired after Margery.

'And what did she say when you told her where I was gone?' said his wife, colouring up as she spoke.

'Why, you must know I did not tell her where you were gone to.'

'You did not!' said she in astonishment; 'then what *did* you tell her?'

'Oh! I merely said you had gone with a neighbour, and you know Mrs. Dawes is not one of the prying sort, so she did not ask where.'

'And pray,' said Margery, looking somewhat archly at her husband, 'what made you so sly about it?'

'I was not sly,' said Carmichael, 'but I was ashamed both of you and myself: of you, that you had gone, and of myself, that I had not influence enough with you to keep you from going.'

The first part of the sentence had begun to raise Margery's wrath, but when she found that her husband blamed himself equally with her, she cooled down, and was just beginning to say, 'What will you bet me that Susan Dawes has

Q

not heard?'—when they were at the door. The
moment Susan came forward to ask them in,
Margery was convinced by her looks that she
had guessed rightly in supposing that some
busybody had informed her of her going astray,
and they had not been long seated before Susan
said, in her dry, yet mild manner, ' So Carmichael
kept your secret yesterday, Margery ; but though
your husband could do so, your *friends* could
not, for I think half a dozen of them at least
have been here to day, each of them actually
buying a pennyworth of something or other, in
order to have the pleasure of telling me that you
had been at their meeting again, after all, and
that they really hoped I would not prevent your
doing so again, for you were certainly less spiritual than you used to be.'

' And what answer did you make them ? ' said
Margery, timidly.

' Why, I told them that *I* had never prevented your going amongst them, for that I had no
power or authority over you ; that I certainly
had told you when you asked my opinion about
attending meetings of all kinds of schism, what
I believed to be the truth, and that I should do
the same again if you asked me ; and, moreover,
I asked them to look at the 14th chapter of St.
Paul's First Epistle to the Corinthians, and at
the 34th and 35th verses, I thought they would
see something which it would appear they had
none of them read, or they would not be trying
to lead you into error as well as themselves.

You surely know the text I mean; and also in his First Epistle to Timothy, at the 11th and 12th verses of the second chapter, he says, "Let the woman learn in silence with all subjection. But I suffer not a woman to teach, nor to usurp authority over the man, but to be in silence."'

'Oh! but,' said Margery, trying to laugh it off, 'I was not teaching, nor preaching, I assure you, so you know *I* was not breaking the Apostle's rule.'

'Oh! Margery, Margery,' said Susan, 'are you really trying to deceive yourself with such a miserable excuse? Have you never read the words, "Be not a partaker in other men's sins," "Follow not a multitude to do evil"?'

'Well,' said Margery, 'I know I've done wrong, and I've felt it the more, because Carmichael has not once scolded me for doing it,.but you may do so as much as you please, and I'll promise to take it well.'

'I have no business to scold anybody,' said Susan, 'but if you feel convinced that you have done wrong, Margery, I'm sure your own feelings will be worse to you than any scoldings from any one; but you must take care that it is something more than a feeling. Probably you had plenty of what I have heard you call "deep feelings" yesterday afternoon, Margery?'

'No, indeed, not so much as I used to have, because you know when Betsy Newtongue was holding forth in the pulpit I could not feel sure that all was right. But, however, there were

some conversions made yesterday, so it seemed
as if some good was done.   There was Sally Jenkins there, who, you know, had scarcely ever
been inside either church or meeting before, and
she declared that she actually felt her sins fall
off, just like chains dropping off her ; but I
think that must have been a fancy, don't you
think so ? '

' Indeed, Margery, I should fear it was a sad
delusion from first to last.   To suppose that a
woman who had lived one of the most wicked
lives that can be imagined should, in one moment,
part with all her sins, is certainly to believe that
we live in an age of miracles, and if such conversions as they are called were to be believed,
we should I fear have even less praying and less
holiness than we have now, for the most wicked
persons would comfort themselves with the idea
that, after indulging in every vice, they might
after all, by just hearing a speech from some
wild fanatic, be turned from darkness to light.
I am sure, Margery, you must see how dangerous such an opinion would be, and how unlike
such a doctrine is to what we are taught by our
blessed Saviour.   He does not tell us that it is
such an easy task to turn from our evil ways.
On the contrary, He tells us that we cannot be
His disciples, unless we take up the cross *daily :*
and that a bad tree cannot bring forth good
fruit.   It must be pruned and watered, before it
can produce good fruit ; and so must the sinner
prune off all his evil habits by the help of God's

Holy Spirit, and all those means which He has given us; but depend upon it, Margery, it must take a long course of repentance and prayer, and diligent reading God's holy word, and a due waiting on all the ordinances of His holy Church, to make one who is grown old in sin turn from a path of guilt to one of righteousness.'

'But,' said Margery, 'they all told me yesterday that we must have "the new birth," or we cannot be saved.'

'Undoubtedly,' said Susan; 'does not the Church, following the Scriptures, tell us this in the Baptismal Service? It teaches us that all human beings are by nature born in sin, and the children of wrath; and that in Baptism we are made members of Christ, the children of God, and inheritors of the kingdom of heaven.

'Our Saviour says to Nicodemus: "Except a man be born of water and of the Spirit, he cannot enter into the kingdom of God."* And again, "He that believeth, and is baptized, shall be saved." You see by this, that baptism must be something more than a mere form; and St. Paul says—"*As many of you as have been baptized into Christ have put on Christ.*" ' †

'Oh, do not give me any more texts,' said Margery, 'but just let Carmichael put down these to talk over with me, for he has a better

---

* John iii. 5.   † Gal. iii. 27.

memory than I have.   I wish I could remember
all you have told me this evening.'

'Ay,' said her husband, 'we must think of
it, and talk of it too, and pray to God to renew
our hearts."

'Yes,' said Susan, 'a humble mind is the
first requisite.   A sense of our ignorance must
produce humility, and a willingness to be
taught, not of man but of God, by His word,
His Church, His ministers, and His ordinances.'

'Ah,' said Margery, '*I* hope I shall not again
wander from the Church, but I hardly dare trust
myself.'

'No, no,' said Carmichael, 'you should *mis*-
trust yourself when you are inclined to run after
Miss Betsy Newtongue again.'

'Oh, I'm not afraid of *her* enticing me,' said
Margery, laughing; 'but then some one else
may, though I hope not.'

Susan kindly said, 'Well, Margery, it is to be
hoped that you won't forget your lesson.   Mine
was more easily learned, because I was taught
in early life to know my baptismal vows, and to
pray to God to enable me to keep them.   Let
us all do this daily, Carmichael, and we shall
not run into any of the follies and disorders of
the day, but we shall daily become more conscious of the blessing of belonging to the Church,
and being taught by her, instead of hanging our
faith on the opinion of any man.'

All this conversation took place some years

ago, and my readers will be pleased to hear that I have had the satisfaction of seeing Carmichael and his wife attending regularly all the services of the Church ; and the change which my sermons had been unable to effect on his intemperance, the grace of God has, I trust, produced ; for I have not a more sober man in my parish, nor more regular communicants than he and Margery. Poor Margery has, I understand, had a good deal of jeering and sarcasm to bear with from her old acquaintances ; but she felt that she was only suffering for her former faults, and she has borne it patiently.

CHAPTER III.

THE postman's knock at Susan's door was always answered with great alacrity by Mary, for the letters he brought were generally either from her dear sailor brother, or her sister Fanny, and she came jumping with delight to her mother to open them. They had always been the bearers of good news, and her youthful heart had not dreamt that any other could be brought by them. It was therefore with her usual glee that Mary skipped round the counter one morning, as she saw the postman turn towards the door.

The letter was speedily paid for (the days of penny stamps had not then arrived), and as quickly put into the hands of her mother; but she soon saw, from the anxious look which spread over her mother's countenance on perusing the letter, that this time at least the postman had not been the bearer of good news. The first page of the sheet was written by Fanny, saying that she had not been well, that she had a cough, and that the doctor thought it would be best for her to try the effect of her native air. The mention of a cough at once alarmed poor Susan, who knew that Fanny had never been one of the strongest. But if Fanny's letter awakened her fears, they were sadly confirmed when she read on the other side the account of her from her mistress, who spoke of her as sadly changed in appearance, and evidently suffering from great weakness. Her mistress added that she had wished Fanny to write, and tell Susan of it some weeks before, but that she delayed from day to day, hoping to find herself better, and fearing to alarm her mother. She begged her to come over as soon as she could conveniently do so, as she did not think it safe for Fanny to travel alone in her present weak state.

Poor Susan could scarcely speak when she had finished her letter; and Mary tried to persuade her mother that it might be merely weakness, and reminded her how rapidly Jane Thompson had recovered when she came home, though the doctors thought her at death's door when she left her place. 'And I'm sure, my dear mother,' she added, 'the very sight of you will do our dear Fan good.' Then she began to enumerate all that she would do for her when they once got her home: that she would go morning and evening at the very time Farmer Lowes's cows were milked, and bring her a cup of new milk, quite warm from the cow; and she would beg Bessie Gray to lend her the donkey she carried the clothes to town on, to give Fanny a ride: and she would make her some of her favourite broth, which she used to say she could take when nothing else would go down (for Fanny never had a healthy appetite); and I do not know how many more kind attentions she would not have enumerated, if Susan had not interrupted her, by kissing her, and saying, 'Yes, Mary, we will do all we can for her, and we must pray for God's blessing on her; but now the first thing to consider is how we shall get her home. If she is as weak as her mistress seems to say she is, she cannot walk from the town here, and indeed I do not know whether she could even walk to the place where the coach passes the end of the village of Oakingtown, for I think it must be a good quarter of a mile from the Grange.' Mary suggested that perhaps it would be better to get a cart and bring her all the way in that. Susan thought the plan a good one, if they could borrow one that went on springs, for she feared the common ones would shake her too much. Mary's active mind soon thought of Tom Bulmer's, and she was presently at his door, telling him how distressed her mother was at the news she had received about her sister, and how anxious she was to bring her home with as little fatigue as possible; and that they thought his spring-cart would answer nicely, if he could spare it, and a man to drive it: 'And mother will gladly pay for both, sir,' said Mary, blushing deeply.

'Thou art a thoughtful lass,' said Bulmer, who was a kind-hearted, blunt farmer, 'and thy mother must have comfort in thee, if she has trouble for thy sister. She shall have the cart, if she wants it, but how to spare her a man, why, I don't know how to manage that; however, I suppose thou art not to be refused, so if I can't spare one, why, I must just go myself for the poor lass. It's a pity, to be sure, to have to bring her from her place, but may be your mother thinks worse of her than she need, and its but natural to be sure. There are few such mothers as yours, Mary, in the parish. I wish there were more, both for the poor bairns' sake and the parish too; for we shouldn't then have so many mischievous lads, and so many useless lasses, as we have now, but we should have some more Mary Daweses, should not we, my lassie?"

Poor Mary knew not how to answer the farmer, but after a minute's hesitation she said:

'Then, sir, may I tell my mother that she can have the cart to fetch Fanny in?'

'Ay, ay; and tell her, too, that I'll go myself, and I'll put a good truss of straw at the bottom of the cart, and that will make it so much the easier for her.'

'Oh! thank you, sir;—I'll run and tell my mother, for she will be so glad. And must she get ready now, sir?'

'As soon as she likes. I'll be at her door in a few minutes.'

Mary ran home as fast as her feet could carry her, and her mother was well pleased at her having executed her mission so well and so promptly; and Susan's bonnet and shawl were soon on, and her old cloak ready to take to wrap round the invalid. She was sitting waiting at the door when farmer Bulmer drew up, and we may be sure she was not long in jumping into the cart beside him; and she immediately began thanking him for his great kindness—but he quickly stopped her, saying that it was nought to talk about, for what were neighbours for, if they were not to serve one another when they wanted a little help?—'I only hope the lass is not as bad as you fancy, and then it will only be a pleasant day's jaunt for you and her, and me too,' said the good-tempered farmer, laughing.

Susan could not join in the laugh, but gave him Fanny's letter (which she had in her pocket) to read. When he had got to the end of it, he said, 'Come, come, Mrs. Dawes, after all it's but a cough, you see, and I've had a cough for this many a year. And it may chance, too, that the poor lass is home-sick, or heart-sick. There's no telling with these lasses how it is.'

Poor Susan shook her head at the good farmer's kind attempt to rally her out of her fears, but she turned the letter over, and pointed to the writing of Fanny's mistress. Farmer Bulmer, who was really a kind-hearted man, saw from the tone of this letter that it was not a matter for jesting, and he felt vexed with himself that he should have spoken so thoughtlessly. 'It's but an ugly account, this, indeed; but there's a God above us, Mrs. Dawes, who orders all for us, and we must e'en submit, for it's not for the like of us mortal men to call Him to account, who it is fit should govern the world as He pleases, since it was He who made it; and somehow or other, if we do try to understand the whys and wherefores of His dealings, we only puzzle our weak brains.'

Poor Susan could only give a short reply to all the farmer's remarks, and he kindly left her to her thoughts till they were within a quarter of a mile of 'The Grange,' and then he told her that she must cheer up, and not let the poor lass see that she had been 'taking on' so, or it would be like enough to kill her at once; and with a thoughtfulness which was scarcely to be expected from one of his rough mould, he said—'Now mind, if she has got thin, and is so much altered as her mistress says, be sure you don't let her observe that you see it, but cheer her up with the thoughts of home, and seeing that nice girl Mary.'

Susan dried up her tears, and tried to assume a composure which she did not feel, and which became more and more difficult the nearer they got to the house. The farmer perceiving this, suggested that they should stop at a cottage in the village, and get a glass of water for her. Susan gladly accepted the proposal, and having relieved her smothered feelings by a flood of tears, drank the cold water, and felt that her nerves were braced up for the trying scene which she felt sure she had to go through. Those only who know what it is to part with one dear to them in all the freshness and vigour of youth, and see them again, after only a few months' absence, pale, emaciated, and prostrate with weakness, can enter into poor Susan's feelings as she approached the bed-side of her daughter. Hard indeed was the struggle to keep down the rising tear, and to conceal the violent beating of the heart; but she did repress the former, and the latter was not perceived by Fanny, who was lying outside of the bed, with the deadly marks of consumption impressed on every feature. There was the bright but painfully glassy eye—the sunken cheek, pale and emaciated, except one spot, which was of a bright hue, and which at once told the sad tale—the feverish hand, the wearing cough, and the voice so changed that Susan had to listen again and again to persuade herself that it was indeed her own Fanny.

The poor girl, whose hurried breathing was made yet quicker by the agitation of seeing her mother, asked her how she was to get home—that she could not walk—that her strength had gone most rapidly—that a week ago she could walk round the garden twice without resting, but that now she believed she could not get to the first flower-bed. She said she longed to be at home with her dear mother and her own Mary, as she always called her (for she had been her chief nurse when a baby), but she knew not how she should get there. When her mother told her that farmer Bulmer had come himself with his spring cart, her bright eye shone yet brighter, and she exclaimed: ' Good, kind farmer Bulmer!—has he really come all this way for me ? Then, dearest mother, let us go ; for I feel as if the *sight* of my own darling Mary would do me good.'

Her mother told her that she should go as soon as they had seen her mistress, who happened to enter the room as she had done speaking. Mrs. Lawrence was very kind to Fanny, and had done all in her power for her ; but she had never seen consumption. She knew nothing of its deadly indications, and although aware of the great change in Fanny's looks and strength, she had no idea that she had to bid farewell to her for ever in this world. Indeed, she had come to Susan

to propose that she should return to her at the end
of three or six months, according to the state of
her health. Susan tried to say, composedly, that
she would let her know how she was going on;
and after putting on Fanny's bonnet and shawl,
they had her lifted into the cart, and by means of a
pillow or two, which her mistress insisted on her
having, they managed to make her a very comfortable bed.

The good farmer was shocked when he saw the
sad change which disease had made in the poor
invalid, but, remembering the lesson he had
given Susan, he said, when she was telling him
how little she could help herself, as he was help-
ing to place her comfortably in the cart : 'Ay,
lass, it's your mother's nursing you want, that's
plain to be seen. We shall see whether that
won't help to bring you about, more than all the
doctor's stuff.'

Poor Fanny looked at her mother as she said,
'Yes, mother, I shall be quite a baby again for
you to nurse and attend to ; and as to Mary,
why we must change places—she must be my
nurse now.'

'You'll have as bonny a nurse, then, as any in
the parish,' said the farmer. 'I believe I should
not mind being ill myself, if I thought I should
get such a nurse.'

Poor Fanny, though too much exhausted to say
more, smiled her thanks for the farmer's high
opinion of Mary, and then resting her head
against her mother, with her pillows to support

her back, she soon fell into a gentle slumber, from which her mother was obliged to rouse her when they approached her house. She thought it would not do for Fanny to wake and find herself at her own door; so she gradually began to change her position, which Fanny immediately feeling, was roused from her sleep, and she asked when her mother was coming. It was evident that she still fancied herself at the Grange, but her mother soon showed her where she was, and told her that before long she would see Mary standing at the door, watching for them to come home. Poor Fanny tried to raise herself up at hearing this, but finding her own weakness, she quietly laid back her head, saying, 'I wonder whether Mary will know her poor Fan.'

The thought had struck Susan before, and she knew not what to do to prepare her for the sad change, for she was sure Mary would be on the watch to receive them. Happily, however, the farmer managed to jump out of the cart in time to warn Mary against going too suddenly to Fanny, and added, 'she's not the lass she was, poor thing, and thou must use all thy gentle ways with her.'

This kind caution prepared Mary a little for what she was to see, but her tears ran fast down her cheeks when she saw her carried into the house, and laid down on the bed quite exhausted by the effort she had made in getting out of the cart. Her mother took Mary aside, and cautioned her against exciting her sister, and poor

Mary, with more resolution than could have been expeeted from one of her tender years, gulped down her tears, and began to beat up an egg with some new milk which she had got a little girl to bring her.. She then seated herself by her side, and as she was looking at her earnestly, Fanny whispered to her that she thought she did not know her.

'To be sure I do, my own Fan,' said Mary, 'but I was thinking what I could do to make you strong again, for I am your nurse now, and you know I must try to learn what is good for you, but I suppose mother will send for the doctor, and he will tell us what to do.'

Susan came into the room at the time, for she had been detained trying to make the good farmer take some money for the loan of the cart, but she might just as well have tried to bring down the church steeple with her single arm, as to get him to take as much as a penny-piece. All she could get from him was,

'I'll take no pay but in kind; when I'm sick you shall come and nurse me, or send my little friend Mary; but till then say nought about it, for what's the day's work of a horse to make such a song about?' and with that he jumped into the cart and drove off as fast as he could. Susan then came into the room where poor Fanny was lying, and was glad to find her more comfortable and composed than she had expected. Mary told her that she had taken all her egg and milk, and Fanny whispered that it was the best thing she had taken for many a day.

R

The next thing to be thought of was sending for the doctor, and Susan said she would go for him whilst Mary remained at her post. Susan accordingly went, and finding Mr. Hammond at home she had the opportunity of telling him, as they walked to the house, the principal things which alarmed her in Fanny's symptoms. The doctor listened attentively to all she told him, occasionally putting a question to her which served to convince her that he, too, thought the case a serious one. Susan, before entering the house, entreated him to give her his candid opinion when he had seen Fanny, which he promised to do, and she knew from experience that she could rely upon him. Mr. Hammond was of course, from his profession, too much accustomed to see the ravages of consumption to show by his manner that he was struck by the change in the appearance of his patient, and she seemed pleased to see him; for having been attended by him as a child, she felt as if she were seeing an old friend, and he kindly took her hand, saying he was sorry that she was come home to be his patient. She looked at him earnestly, and then with a faint smile said, ' Then you don't like to have patients.'

The doctor smiled at the quickness of her reply, and said, ' Why, Fanny, it is painful even to hard-hearted doctors (as we are sometimes called) to witness suffering, but, however, when we can relieve it, it is some compensation to us; and now I must not tire you with talking about doctors or patients (excepting yourself), as I want to hear all about your illness."

Poor Fanny soon found that talking of that was sufficient to wear her out, and after telling how suddenly she had lost all her strength, and showing her wasted arms, she was seized with a fit of coughing which showed Mr. Hammond in a few minutes her real state. When the fit was over, he told her not to speak again for fear of causing a return, but promised to tell her mother all he wished her to do. As he left the room, he charged Mary to beware of draughts of air; and, as if acting on his own orders, shut the door very quietly, Susan having preceded him out of the room. As soon as he had gone far enough off from the wall to prevent Fanny from hearing what was passing, he said to Susan, who was dreading to ask his opinion,

'Well, Mrs. Dawes, I am sure you are prepared for my opinion. No one can look at that poor girl, with that deceitful bloom on her cheek, without feeling that she is not to come to maturity in this world. All the alleviation that I can give her you may be sure I will; but it would be cruelty in me, were I to buoy you up with any hopes of my doing her any permanent good.'

Susan's tears streamed apace as the doctor proceeded, and he saw that she could make no reply, so he went on to say, that she must avoid all excitement, as anything of that kind would in all probability materially hasten her departure. He enjoined the greatest attention to be paid to keeping her mind calm and composed, and recommended new milk, and everything of a light and nourishing nature, as the best medicine she could take: in fact, he said, he should send her nothing but a little soothing syrup, when her cough was troublesome. Susan did not dare to go into the next room for some little time, as she felt sure that Fanny would immediately perceive that she had been crying, and it was fortunate that, whilst she was sitting in the shop waiting till she could venture to go back again, Margaret arrived to inquire how Fanny was, Mary having sent her word in the morning that she was coming home on that day. Margaret, little fancying that Fanny's illness was of a kind to cause her mother alarm, was distressed at seeing her countenance so full of grief as she opened the door of the shop. She went up gently to her, entreating to know the cause of it. Her mother motioned to her to be quiet, and then commenced telling her as well as she could of poor Fanny's state, and the doctor's opinion of her.

'But doctors are not always right, my dear mother,' said Margaret, 'and I hope that Mr. Hammond will be wrong this once.'

'Wait, Margaret, till you see what a wreck she is of what she once was, and then see, if even you with your naturally hopeful temper can give me any hope. No, no, I feel certain that God will call her to himself at no distant time, and all I pray for is that she may be fit to go to Him, and that I may be prepared to part with her.'

Margaret, to great natural spirits, united a warm and feeling heart : and nothing distressed her so much as the sight of her mother in trouble, and, unlike her youthful sister Mary, her sobs could not be repressed in a moment, so her mother took her into a neighbour's house till she could compose herself, and there left her whilst she went back to Fanny. As soon as she had seated herself on her bed, Fanny took her by the hand, and said, ' You've had a long talk with the doctor, what does he think of me ? ' Her mother told her she had not been talking much to the doctor, but that Margaret had arrived, and she had been talking to her.'

. ' And why does she not come to see me ? ' said Fanny, becoming more excited than her mother liked to see her.

' Because, my dear Fanny, I wished to come and tell you she was here first, and to see whether you were strong enough to see her now, for your doctor says you must not see any one when you feel fatigued.'

' Oh ! but I must see my dear sister.'

' Then you must promise not to talk, my dear girl, for I see you are tired.' Saying so, Susan left the room, and soon returned with Margaret, who behaved with more calmness, at first seeing her, than could have been expected, though the constant change in the colour of her cheeks showed that she was under strong excitement, and she soon made an excuse to leave Fanny, by saying that her Mistress would be wanting her,

and she would ask leave in a day or two to come
and see her again.　Fanny, who was really worn
out with all the exertion of the day, bid her good
night.

When Margaret returned home she immediately came to my wife, (for she was still our
servant,) to tell her that she was sure Fanny was
dying ; and when she told her of all her sad
symptoms, my wife could not but agree with her
that it was to be feared it would terminate fatally,
endeavouring, at the same time, to soothe Margaret, (whose sobs had called me to the room they
were in,) by telling her she would let her go and
see her sister as often as possible, and that she
must try and help to support her mother in this
new trial, and not give way to grief, which would
soon make her useless.　I advised my wife to
leave her to herself for a quarter of an hour, that
she might give free vent to her tears, as I felt sure
she was suffering from having been obliged to
restrain them before her sister.　My wife returned at the end of that time, and gently opened
the door which she had left slightly ajar, and
hearing no sound she went in, and there saw
Margaret kneeling by the bed-side, her head
completely buried in her pocket-handkerchief,
so that she retreated without Margaret being
aware that any one had been in the room.　A
short time after she returned and found her
much more composed ; her eyes indeed were red
and swollen with crying, but she was able to
swallow a glass of wine.　My wife recommended

her to go to bed, promising that she should spend the following afternoon with her sister, if her mother wished her to do so.

I called the next morning to inquire after the poor sufferer, and found that she had had a very uncomfortable night; her mind constantly wandering, and fancying that her mother was not with her. I did not ask to see her, for I thought perhaps she was not strong enough, but Susan said she would be sure to hear my voice, for she was so quick in recognising voices, and she thought perhaps that she had better tell her, and see if she would wish me to go in. She said, 'yes,' and that 'I must offer up some prayers for her, for she could not go to church now.'

Susan begged me not to stay long, and not to allow her to talk much, for she was soon tired. Her eye shone bright with consumption's deceitful lustre, and she seemed to exert herself to welcome me, but I told her that I was under orders not to allow her to talk much.

'But I must ask you to pray for me,' said she, 'for I am very, very weak, Mr. Wilson; God can raise me up again, I know, but I think no doctor can, though Mr. Hammond is very kind. I can't get to church now; sometimes I can't even say my prayers in bed, but you will say them for me.'

Her manner became hurried as she spoke, and I felt anxious to make her leave off talking, so I asked her if I should do so now.

'Yes, pray do; but, Mr. Wilson, I am very

weak; and pray for me whenever you have prayers in church that if it shall be God's holy will, He may, for Jesus Christ's sake, give me my health again.'

I immediately knelt down and used a prayer or two, from the service for the Visitation of the Sick, but before I had finished, she had sunk into a sweet sleep: I therefore left the room as quietly as I could. Susan followed me into her shop, and then with some hesitation asked me what I thought of her dear Fanny. I told her that it seemed to me as if there could be but one opinion of her.

'Ah!' she said, 'I fear so, but you will come and see her again, Mr. Wilson?'

'Oh, certainly, I will call and hear how she is, and if she can bear it I will read to her; but it strikes me, Susan, that she is not able to bear much reading, and unless she rallies, which she may do, perhaps, for a time, we must do nothing that will in any way excite her.'

Susan was much overcome at what I said, but tried to say something about her receiving the Holy Communion.

'If she should express a wish to receive it,' I said, 'I will come to her at any time to administer it, but you may be thankful that you have no cause for anxiety about her if she does not.

'No, Sir, I trust not; at least in health she never missed attending the Lord's Table when it was prepared; it is now five years since she was confirmed, and I think she has never since then

missed an opportunity of receiving the Communion.'

'Well, Susan, then,' I replied, 'you may well
find comfort in thinking that during five years
of health she has not neglected this needful duty.
Far more satisfactory must your reflections be
under such circumstances, than if she had sent
for me at the last to administer to her that
spiritual food which in health she had rejected.'

Susan tried to say something, but I saw she
could not; and feeling that my presence and
conversation were adding to her emotion, I bade
her good-bye, assuring her that Fanny should be
remembered in our prayers at church the following morning, which was Sunday.

As soon as Susan had sufficiently recovered
herself to return to the invalid's room she did so,
and found her still dozing. The watchful mother
had not been long in the room, when the cough,
the sure attendant of this insidious disease, roused
her from her slumbers; and, as if unconscious of
the time that had passed, she asked why Mr.
Wilson did not go on with the prayer.

When her mother explained to her that I had
gone while she slept, she said, 'Oh! well, to-
morrow is Sunday, he'll pray for me in church
then.' Mary nodded her assent, and slipped out of
the room, her mother having begged her to make
Fanny a little arrow-root, for she saw that she
wanted an excuse to go out of the room and
give vent to her feelings. She soon returned
with the arrow-root, and was pleased to see

Fanny enjoy a few spoonsful of it. It was very little that she could take at a time, and she often tried to swallow a little merely to please Mary.

When I visited the poor sufferer again I found her very much changed for the worse. Her cough was incessant, her breathing much more hurried, and her poor little hand burnt up with fever. As I sat down by her side, she gave me a gentle smile, and said, 'You see your prayers have not been heard for my body, but you must pray for my soul ; and you must tell mother and Mary not to cry so.'

At this Mary quitted the room, and left me alone with Fanny. She stopped between every two or three words, as if to take breath, and after a long pause she said, 'When is Whit-Sunday, Mr. Wilson ? I don't know the days now.'

'The Sunday after next,' I replied, 'will be Whit-Sunday.'

She seemed to think earnestly for a few minutes, and I did not speak till she broke the silence, by saying, 'I have a favour to ask you, Mr. Wilson ;' and then, in a lower tone, she added, 'perhaps the last.'

'I am sure,' I replied, 'that I shall have pleasure in granting it, if I can do so.'

Her eyes brightened as I spoke, and a sweet smile shone on her countenance as she said : 'I have always received the Holy Communion on that day since I was confirmed.'

Here she stopped again, as if wanting breath ;

and in order to give her time to rest, and guessing her request, I said : ' Yes, Fanny, and so I suppose you wish to receive it next Whit-Sunday : is that your request ? if so, I can promise very readily to comply with it.'

'Thank you, oh ! thank you,' she said, with more strength of voice than I had fancied she possessed ; and then after a pause, ' I know you are very busy on a Sunday with the services of the church, as well as with the schools, but I do not think that I shall long add to your troubles. Do not, Sir, tell my mother so : you see how thin I am,'—and she showed me her withered hand and wrist. ' Do you think,' she added, ' that it is consumption ? I think it must be, for I am just as Mary Lawson was, sometimes better, and then I talk as she did about getting well, but I do not think I can, when I look at myself ; do you, Mr. Wilson ? '

I scarcely knew how to answer her. I could only say : ' You know, Fanny, God can raise you even from the bed of death, if it be His will, and whilst there is life there is hope ; meanwhile, you cannot but be safe in resigning yourself to His will.'

She gently raised her hand once or twice, saying, in a low tone scarcely above a whisper, ' Pray for me.' I was glad to do so, and after a short prayer, Mary came in. As I saw that Fanny wanted rest, I told Mary that she must not let her talk ; and, promising to see her again

before Whit-Sunday, I took her by the hand,
and gave her my blessing.

Susan was in the shop serving some customers,
but I waited till they had finished their purchases,
and then told Susan of poor Fanny's wish to
receive the Holy Communion on Whit-Sunday.

Susan then inquired whether I should object
to her daughter Margaret and her son James
receiving the Communion with her. 'My dear
sailor,' she added, with a sigh, 'will not, I fear,
be at home to join with us in this last family
Communion on earth.'

I told Susan I could have no objection to their
doing so, as I knew they were in the habit of
attending the Lord's Table.

As I felt convinced, from Fanny's appearance,
that she would not number many more weeks
on earth, we sent Margaret to be with her constantly by day, to relieve her mother and Mary,
who sat up alternately at night with her. James
could only get over to see her on a Sunday, but
he was sure to bring her some little thing which
he hoped would tempt her to eat. The whole of
the following week Fanny's chief talk was about
the approaching Whit-Sunday.

But before Whit-Sunday had arrived, her
spirit had joined, we may humbly hope, the
communion of saints in another world.

On the Friday previous I had seen her; and
although experience ought to have taught me
how deceitful often is that rallying of strength

and spirit shortly before death, I left her, I confess, without any apprehension of her being
summoned before the following Sunday. A few
hours, however, only had elapsed, from the time
of my leaving her, before she sunk into a sweet
sleep, from which she never awoke in this
world. So calm, so quiet, so entirely without
struggle was her change, that it was some time
before her mother and Mary could persuade
themselves that her spirit indeed had taken its
flight. Margaret was not with her at the time,
for when she saw how calmly she was sleeping,
she bade her mother and sister good-night, feeling happy that she left Fanny so comfortable.
They did not send for her till the morning,
knowing that she could do no good, and that
a night's rest would fit her the better for the sad
duties of the next day. Early on the following
morning they sent her word that she must not
expect to see her sister alive. Poor Margaret
turned deadly pale as she received the intelli-
gence, and ran to me to ask me to go with her;
but, as I had heard from the messenger pre-
viously that all was over, and had charged
our servant not to tell her so abruptly, I told
her I would follow her if her mother sent back
the messenger for me. One of the servants
walked with her; and the closed shutters soon
showed that death had made its abode in that
house.

A kind neighbour, to whom Susan had formerly been of great service during the illness of

her husband, opened the door very gently; and the dim light disclosed the figures of Mary and her mother standing at the foot of the bed where Fanny's corpse lay. A few primroses were strewn over the bed, and her countenance was so much like what it had been in health, that Margaret was quite overcome at the sight. Even the slight bloom had not left the cheek, and the calmness and sweetness was so like that of sleep, that it was hard indeed to persuade oneself that it was a sleep from which she would awake no more in this world. Her face was the only part of her that had not become painfully emaciated, and certainly, as she lay in her coffin, I thought I had never seen repose more beautifully depicted on any countenance. Susan wished me to come and take a last look at her, for she felt that on the Friday I had not bidden her 'farewell.'

The funeral was fixed for Wednesday. Poor James, who came over as soon as he heard of his sister's death, remained with his mother till the interment, and it was pleasing to see in so young a man so much thoughtful consideration for his mother. By being beforehand in ordering the necessaries for the funeral, he saved her much trouble and pain. The particulars of the funeral I am sure I need not give. My readers may imagine a large concourse of the young following Fanny to the church, and then to the grave. The attendance of these young persons was unasked: they came uninvited save by their own hearts, which prompted them to mingle their tears together on the loss of their former friend. Susan, Margaret, and Mary were there, listening to those blessed words of consolation, ' I am the resurrection and the life, saith the Lord; he that believeth in me, though he were dead, yet shall he live, and whosoever liveth and believeth in me shall never die.' A faint ' Amen ' was repeated by Susan, when the clergyman said, ' The Lord gave, and the Lord hath taken away, blessed be the name of the Lord.' The prayers affected them all deeply, and at one time I feared that Margaret must have left the grave. But she remained till the last; and James and their old friend Simpson (who was the only stranger at the funeral excepting two young friends of Fanny) conducted Susan and her two daughters safely home, and left them in the evening, calm and composed.

I saw Susan a few days afterwards, looking much as usual. Her cheek was perhaps a shade paler and her manner more subdued; but she could talk of Fanny without strong emotion, and seemed to feel deeply thankful for the calmness of her end, and the happy state in which she had died. Nothing, perhaps, has tried her more than the return of her sailor son, who, having heard no tidings even of the illness of his sister, came home unconscious of his loss. He was struck with his mother's manner when she came to meet him with tears in her eyes, not indeed of joy, as on former occasions, but of suffering.   Mary's black gown next alarmed him, and he begged them to tell him what it all meant.

Poor fellow! his honest sailor's joy at returning home, after an absence of eighteen months, was indeed changed into mourning, and he could do nothing but talk of poor Fanny's illness for the remainder of the day.   He had but a few weeks to be at home before his next voyage, so that Susan felt bound not to depress him more than she could help; but he would pay a visit every evening to the grave of his sister, and at his own expense had a little tablet put up to her memory, which is now in my church.   He felt more at parting with his mother the next voyage than he had ever done before.   He had never known till now what it was to leave all well, and to return and find one gone.   He felt now that he knew not who might be the next to be taken, and as he gave his mother his last embrace, he offered a fervent prayer that God would preserve her and all dear to him.   In this prayer he is joined by many in the village, and by none more sincerely than myself, who daily feel more and more that no person in the parish would be more missed than Susan Dawes

THE END.

JOHN CHILDS AND SON, PRINTERS.

Society
FOR
Promoting Christian Knowledge.

BOOKS SUITABLE FOR PRESENTS.

Most of these Works may be had in ornamental bindings, with gilt edges, at an extra charge of 6d. each.

	Price. s.	d.
AFRICAN KINGDOMS and PEOPLES, Sketches of the, with Map.	4	0
ALICE GRAY; or, the Ministrations of a Child . .	2	0
AMY'S TRIALS; or, a Character Misunderstood . .	2	0
ARTHUR; or, the Chorister's Rest	1	0
BIBLE PICTURES and STORIES. With Colored Plates. In 2 Vols. . . . . *each*	3	0
BIRDS of the SEA-SHORE. 12 Colored Plates . .	1	8
BIRDS' NESTS, with 22 Colored Plates of Eggs. By the Rev. C. A. JOHNS	4	6
BRITISH SETTLEMENTS in INDIA, History of	4	0
BRITISH FISHES, A Familiar History of	4	0
BRITISH BUTTERFLIES. Colored Plates . . .	1	8
BROKEN ARM, The	2	6
CHANNEL ISLANDS, Rambles among the . . .	3	0
CHAPTERS on COMMON THINGS of the SEA-SIDE. By ANNE PRATT	4	0
CHEMISTRY of CREATION	5	0
(*Demy* 18*mo.*)		

BOOKS SUITABLE FOR PRESENTS.

BOOKS SUITABLE FOR PRESENTS.

BOOKS SUITABLE FOR PRESENTS.

	Price. s. d.
SHORT STORIES founded on EUROPEAN HISTORY.—FRANCE, ITALY, SPAIN, SWEDEN, SWITZERLAND . . . . *each*	2 0
SISTERS, The. By Mrs. Tomlinson	2 0
SKETCHES of RURAL AFFAIRS	3 6
STORIES from ROMAN HISTORY	3 0
———— for the NURSERY	2 6
TEACHERS and TAUGHT	1 0
TEMPEST, The; or, an Account of the Nature, Properties, Dangers, and Uses of Wind in various Parts of the World. New Edition	3 6
TEXT BOOK of ZOOLOGY. By P. H. Gosse, F.R.S.	3 6
THUNDER-STORM, The. By C. Tomlinson, Esq. New Edition. Fcap. 8vo.	3 6
TRAVELS by LAND and SEA; The Old Arm Chair, or	3 0
TWINS, The; or, Home Scenes	1 8
TWO FIRESIDES, The. A Tale	2 0
WILD FLOWERS. By Anne Pratt. 2 Vols. 192 Colored Plates	16 0
YEAR of COUNTRY LIFE; or, Chronicle of the Young Naturalists	2 6

An Allowance of 25 per Cent. to Members.

DEPOSITORIES:
77, Great Queen Street, Lincoln's Inn Fields ; 4, Royal Exchange ; 16, Hanover Street, Hanover Square.

CPSIA information can be obtained
at www.ICGtesting.com
Printed in the USA
BVHW091901220819
556561BV00021B/5021/P